# Microsoft® PowerPoint® 2000
## Brief Edition

# INTERACTIVE COMPUTING SERIES

Kenneth C. Laudon
Kenneth Rosenblatt

*Azimuth Interactive, Inc.*

Boston    Burr Ridge, IL    Dubuque, IA    Madison, WI    New York    San Francisco    St. Louis
Bangkok    Bogotá    Caracas    Lisbon    London    Madrid    Mexico City    Milan    New Delhi    Seoul
Singapore    Sydney    Taipei    Toronto

## McGraw-Hill Higher Education

*A Division of The* **McGraw-Hill** *Companies*

ISBN   0-07-234078-9

Vice president/Editor-in-Chief:   *Michael W. Junior*
Sponsoring editor:   *Trisha O'Shea*
Developmental editor:   *Kyle Thomes*
Senior marketing manager:   *Jodi McPherson*
Project manager:   *Carrie Sestak*
Production supervisor:   *Michael R. McCormick*
Senior freelance design coordinator:   *Laurie Entringer*
Supplement coordinator:   *Matthew Perry*
Compositor:   *Azimuth Interactive, Inc.*
Typeface:   *10/12 Sabon*
Printer:   *Quebecor Printing Book Group/Dubuque*

Library of Congress Catalog Card Number: 99-63168

http://www.mhhe.com

# Microsoft® PowerPoint® 2000
## Brief Edition

# INTERACTIVE COMPUTING SERIES

Kenneth C. Laudon
Kenneth Rosenblatt

*Azimuth Interactive, Inc.*

At **McGraw-Hill Higher Education**, we publish instructional materials targeted at the higher education market. In an effort to expand the tools of higher learning, we publish texts, lab manuals, study guides, testing materials, software, and multimedia products.

At **Irwin/McGraw-Hill** (a division of McGraw-Hill Higher Education), we realize technology will continue to create new mediums for professors and students to manage resources and communicate information with one another. We strive to provide the most flexible and complete teaching and learning tools available and offer solutions to the changing world of teaching and learning.

**Irwin/McGraw-Hill is dedicated to providing the tools necessary for today's instructors and students to navigate the world of Information Technology successfully.**

**Seminar Series** - Irwin/McGraw-Hill's Technology Connection seminar series offered across the country every year, demonstrates the latest technology products and encourages collaboration among teaching professionals.

**Osborne/McGraw-Hill** - A division of the McGraw-Hill Companies known for its best-selling Internet titles *Harley Hahn's Internet & Web Yellow Pages* and the *Internet Complete Reference*, offers an additional resource for certification and has strategic publishing relationships with corporations such as Corel Corporation and America Online. For more information, visit Osborne at www.osborne.com.

**Digital Solutions** - Irwin/McGraw-Hill is committed to publishing Digital Solutions. Taking your course online doesn't have to be a solitary venture. Nor does it have to be a difficult one. We offer several solutions, which will let you enjoy all the benefits of having course material online. For more information, visit www.mhhe.com/solutions/index.mhtml.

**Packaging Options** - For more about our discount options, contact your local Irwin/McGraw-Hill Sales representative at 1-800-338-3987, or visit our Web site at www.mhhe.com/it.

# *Preface*

## Interactive Computing Series

### Goals/Philosophy

The *Interactive Computing Series* provides you with an illustrated interactive environment for learning software skills using Microsoft Office. The Interactive Computing Series is composed of both text and multimedia interactive CD-ROMs. The text and the CD-ROMs are closely coordinated. *It's up to you. You can choose how you want to learn.*

### Approach

The *Interactive Computing Series* is the visual interactive way to develop and apply software skills. This skills-based approach coupled with its highly visual, two-page spread design allows the student to focus on a single skill without having to turn the page. A running case study is provided through the text, reinforcing the skills and giving a real-world focus to the learning process.

**About the Book**

The Interactive Computing Series offers *two levels* of instruction. Each level builds upon the previous level.

**Brief lab manual** - covers the basics of the application, contains two to four chapters.
**Introductory lab manual** - includes the material in the Brief textbook plus two to four additional chapters. The Introductory lab manuals prepare students for the *Microsoft Office User Specialist Proficiency Exam (MOUS Certification)*.

Each lesson is organized around **Skills, Concepts,** and **Steps (Do It!).**

Each lesson is divided into a number of Skills. Each **Skill** is first explained at the top of the page.
Each **Concept** is a concise description of why the skill is useful and where it is commonly used.
Each **Step (Do It!)** contains the instructions on how to complete the skill.

**About the CD-ROM**

The CD-ROM provides a unique interactive environment for students where they learn to use software faster and remember it better. The CD-ROM is organized in a similar approach as the text: The **Skill** is defined, the **Concept** is explained in rich multimedia, and the student performs **Steps (Do It!)** within sections called Interactivities. There are at least 45 Interactivities per CD-ROM. Some of the features of the CD-ROM are:

**Simulated Environment** - The Interactive Computing CD-ROM places students in a simulated controlled environment where they can practice and perform the skills of the application software.
**Interactive Exercises** - The student is asked to demonstrate command of a specific software skill. The student's actions are followed by a digital "TeacherWizard" that provides feedback.
**SmartQuizzes** - Provide performance-based assessment of the student at the end of each lesson.

# *Using the Book*

In the book, each skill is described in a two-page graphical spread (Figure 1). The left side of the two-page spread describes the skill, the concept, and the steps needed to perform the skill. The right side of the spread uses screen shots to show you how the screen should look at key stages.

Figure 1

Skill: Each lesson is divided into a number of specific skills

Concept: A concise description of why the skill is useful and where it is commonly used

Running case: A real-world case ties the skill and the concept to a practical situation

Do It!: Step-by-step directions show you how to use the skill

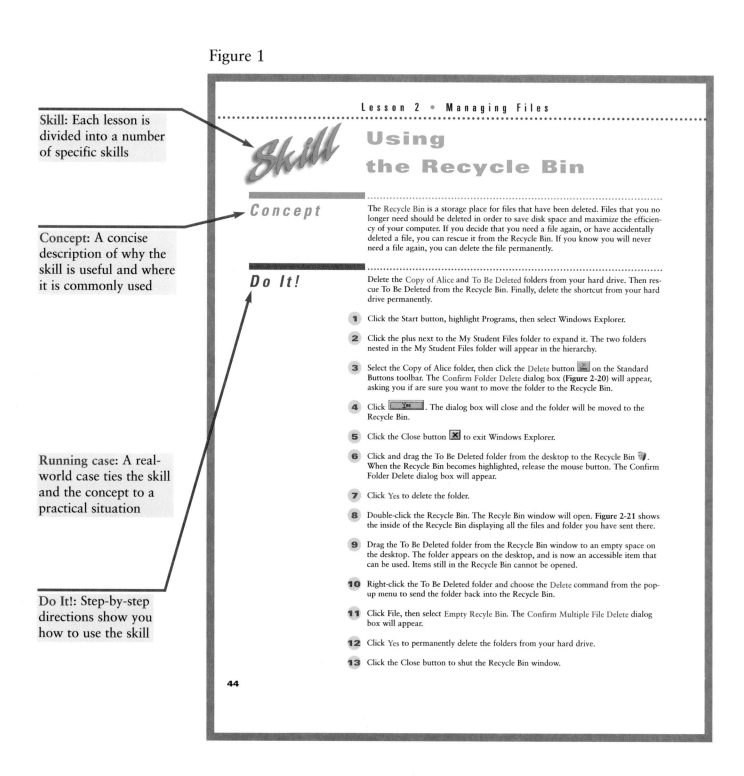

Lesson 2 • Managing Files

## *Skill* Using the Recycle Bin

*Concept*

The Recycle Bin is a storage place for files that have been deleted. Files that you no longer need should be deleted in order to save disk space and maximize the efficiency of your computer. If you decide that you need a file again, or have accidentally deleted a file, you can rescue it from the Recycle Bin. If you know you will never need a file again, you can delete the file permanently.

*Do It!*

Delete the Copy of Alice and To Be Deleted folders from your hard drive. Then rescue To Be Deleted from the Recycle Bin. Finally, delete the shortcut from your hard drive permanently.

1. Click the Start button, highlight Programs, then select Windows Explorer.

2. Click the plus next to the My Student Files folder to expand it. The two folders nested in the My Student Files folder will appear in the hierarchy.

3. Select the Copy of Alice folder, then click the Delete button on the Standard Buttons toolbar. The Confirm Folder Delete dialog box (**Figure 2-20**) will appear, asking you if are sure you want to move the folder to the Recycle Bin.

4. Click Yes. The dialog box will close and the folder will be moved to the Recycle Bin.

5. Click the Close button to exit Windows Explorer.

6. Click and drag the To Be Deleted folder from the desktop to the Recycle Bin. When the Recycle Bin becomes highlighted, release the mouse button. The Confirm Folder Delete dialog box will appear.

7. Click Yes to delete the folder.

8. Double-click the Recycle Bin. The Recyle Bin window will open. **Figure 2-21** shows the inside of the Recycle Bin displaying all the files and folder you have sent there.

9. Drag the To Be Deleted folder from the Recycle Bin window to an empty space on the desktop. The folder appears on the desktop, and is now an accessible item that can be used. Items still in the Recycle Bin cannot be opened.

10. Right-click the To Be Deleted folder and choose the Delete command from the pop-up menu to send the folder back into the Recycle Bin.

11. Click File, then select Empty Recycle Bin. The Confirm Multiple File Delete dialog box will appear.

12. Click Yes to permanently delete the folders from your hard drive.

13. Click the Close button to shut the Recycle Bin window.

44

## End-of-Lesson Features

In the book, the learning in each lesson is reinforced at the end by a quiz and a skills review called Interactivity, which provides step-by-step exercises and real-world problems for the students to solve independently.

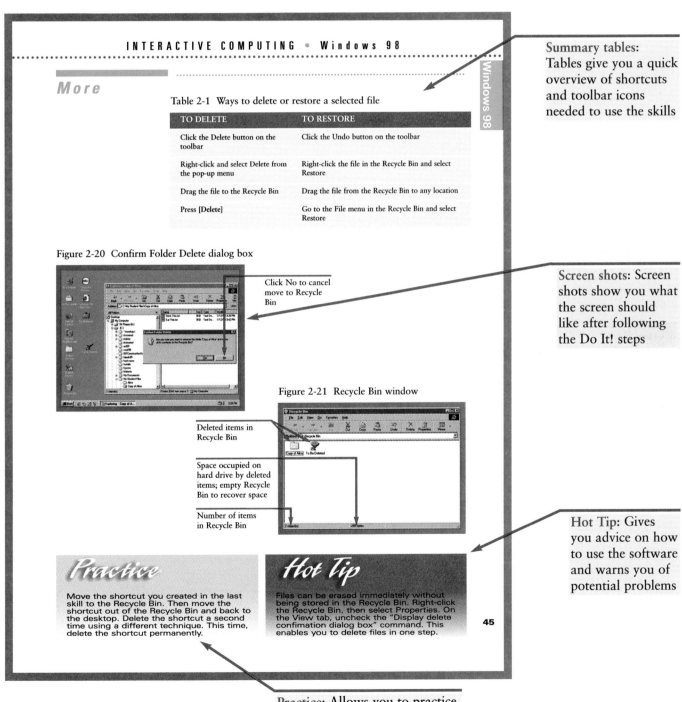

INTERACTIVE COMPUTING • Windows 98

Windows 98

*More*

Table 2-1 Ways to delete or restore a selected file

| TO DELETE | TO RESTORE |
|---|---|
| Click the Delete button on the toolbar | Click the Undo button on the toolbar |
| Right-click and select Delete from the pop-up menu | Right-click the file in the Recycle Bin and select Restore |
| Drag the file to the Recycle Bin | Drag the file from the Recycle Bin to any location |
| Press [Delete] | Go to the File menu in the Recycle Bin and select Restore |

Figure 2-20 Confirm Folder Delete dialog box

Click No to cancel move to Recycle Bin

Figure 2-21 Recycle Bin window

Deleted items in Recycle Bin

Space occupied on hard drive by deleted items; empty Recycle Bin to recover space

Number of items in Recycle Bin

*Practice*

Move the shortcut you created in the last skill to the Recycle Bin. Then move the shortcut out of the Recycle Bin and back to the desktop. Delete the shortcut a second time using a different technique. This time, delete the shortcut permanently.

*Hot Tip*

Files can be erased immediately without being stored in the Recycle Bin. Right-click the Recycle Bin, then select Properties. On the View tab, uncheck the "Display delete confimation dialog box" command. This enables you to delete files in one step.

45

Summary tables: Tables give you a quick overview of shortcuts and toolbar icons needed to use the skills

Screen shots: Screen shots show you what the screen should like after following the Do It! steps

Hot Tip: Gives you advice on how to use the software and warns you of potential problems

Practice: Allows you to practice the skill with a built-in exercise or directs you to a student file

# Using the Interactive CD-ROM

The Interactive Computing multimedia CD-ROM provides an unparalleled learning environment in which you can learn software skills faster and better than in books alone. The CD-ROM creates a unique interactive environment in which you can learn to use software faster and remember it better. The CD-ROM uses the same lessons, skills, concepts, and Do It! steps as found in the book, but presents the material using voice, video, animation, and precise simulation of the software you are learning. A typical CD-ROM contents screen shows the major elements of a lesson (see Figure 2 below).

Skills list: A list of skills allows you to jump directly to any skill you want to learn or review, including interactive sessions with the TeacherWizard

Figure 2

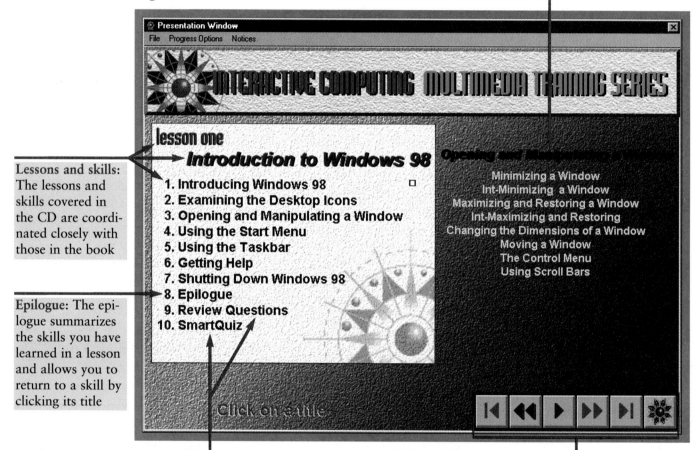

Lessons and skills: The lessons and skills covered in the CD are coordinated closely with those in the book

Epilogue: The epilogue summarizes the skills you have learned in a lesson and allows you to return to a skill by clicking its title

Review Questions and SmartQuiz: Review Questions test your knowledge of the concepts covered in the lesson; SmartQuiz tests your ability to accomplish tasks in a simulated software environment

User controls: Precise and simple user controls permit you to start, stop, pause, jump forward or backward one sentence, or jump forward or backward an entire skill. A single navigation star takes you back to the lesson's table of contents

# Unique Features of the CD-ROM: TeacherWizard™ and SmartQuiz™

*Interactive Computing: Software Skills* offers many leading-edge features on the CD currently found in no other learning product on the market. One such feature is *interactive exercises* in which you are asked to demonstrate your command of a software skill in a precisely simulated software environment. Your actions are followed closely by a digital TeacherWizard that guides you with additional information if you make a mistake. When you complete the action called for by the TeacherWizard correctly, you are congratulated and prompted to continue the lesson. If you make a mistake, the TeacherWizard gently lets you know: "No, that's not the right icon. Click on the Folder icon on the left side of the top toolbar to open a file." No matter how many mistakes you make, the TeacherWizard is there to help you.

Another leading-edge feature is the end-of-lesson SmartQuiz. Unlike the multiple choice and matching questions found in the book quiz, the SmartQuiz puts you in a simulated digital software world and asks you to show your mastery of skills while actually working with the software (Figure 3).

Figure 3

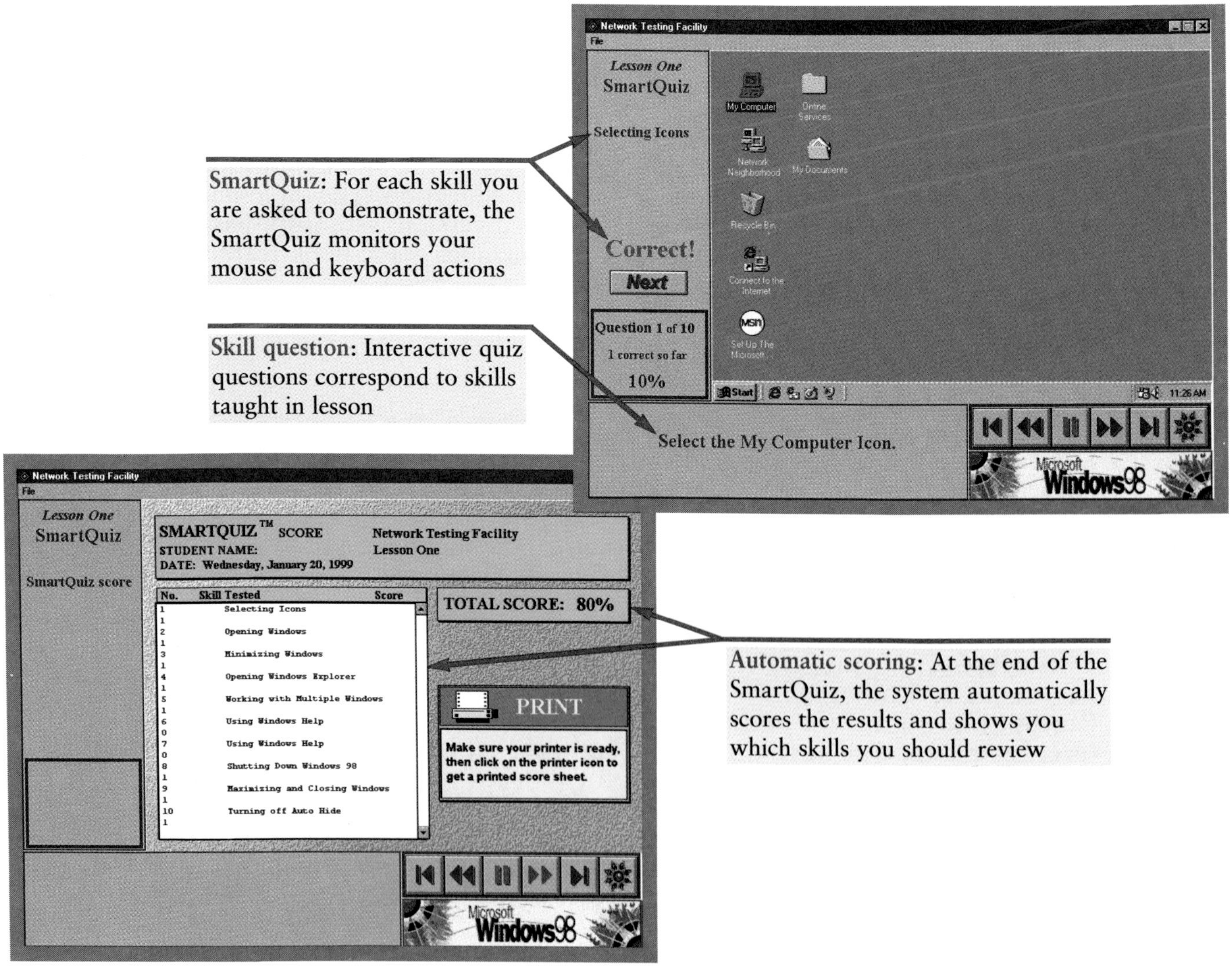

SmartQuiz: For each skill you are asked to demonstrate, the SmartQuiz monitors your mouse and keyboard actions

Skill question: Interactive quiz questions correspond to skills taught in lesson

Automatic scoring: At the end of the SmartQuiz, the system automatically scores the results and shows you which skills you should review

# Teaching Resources

The following is a list of supplemental material available with the Interactive Computing Series:

ATLAS Active Testing and Learning Assessment Software - available for the Interactive Computing Series, is our cutting edge "Real TimeAssessment" software. ATLAS is web-enabled and allows students to perform timed tasks while working live in an application. ATLAS will track how a specific task is completed and the time it takes to complete that task. ATLAS measures Proficiency and Efficiency ("It's not only what you do but how you do it."). ATLAS will provide full customization and authoring capabilities for professors, and includes content from all of our application Series.

## Instructor's Resource Kits

The Instructor's Resource Kit provides professors with all of the ancillary material needed to teach a course. Irwin/McGraw-Hill is dedicated to providing instructors with the most effective instruction resources available. Many of these resources are available at our Information Technology Supersite www.mhhe.com/it. Our Instructor's Kits are available on CD-ROM and contain the following:

> Network Testing Facility (NTF) - Tests acquired software skills in a safe simulated software environment. NTF tracks a student score and allows the instructor to build screens that indicate student progress.
> Diploma by Brownstone - is the most flexible, powerful, and easy-to-use computerized testing system available in higher education. The diploma system allows professors to create an Exam as a printed version, as a LAN-based Online version, and as an Internet version. Diploma includes grade book features, which automate the entire testing process.
> Instructor's Manual - Includes:
> -Solutions to all lessons and end-of-unit material
> -Teaching Tips
> -Teaching Strategies
> -Additional exercises.
> Student Data Files - To use the Interactive Computing Series, students must have Student Data Files to complete practice and test sessions. The instructor and students using this text in classes are granted the right to post the student files on any network or stand-alone computer, or to distribute the files on individual diskettes. The student files may be downloaded from our IT Supersite at www.mhhe.com/it.
> Series Web Site - Available at www.mhhe.com/cit/apps/laudon.

## Digital Solutions

> Pageout Lite - is designed if you're just beginning to explore Web site options. Pageout Lite is great for posting your own material online. You may choose one of three templates, type in your material, and Pageout Lite instantly converts it to HTML.
> Pageout - is our Course Web site Development Center. Pageout offers a Syllabus page, Web site address, Online Learning Center Content, online exercises and quizzes, gradebook, discussion board, an area for students to build their own Web pages, and all the features of Pageout Lite. For more information please visit the Pageout Web site at www.mhla.net/pageout.

## Teaching Resources (continued)

OLC/Series Web Sites - Online Learning Centers (OLCs)/Series Sites are accessible through our Supersite at www.mhhe.com/it. Our Online Learning Centers/Series Sites provide pedagogical features and supplements for our titles online. Students can point and click their way to key terms, learning objectives, chapter overviews, PowerPoint slides, exercises, and web links.

The McGraw-Hill Learning Architecture (MHLA) - is a complete course delivery system. MHLA gives professors ownership in the way digital content is presented to the class through online quizzing, student collaboration, course administration, and content management. For a walk-through of MHLA visit the MHLA Web site at www.mhla.net.

Packaging Options - For more about our discount options, contact your local Irwin/McGraw-Hill Sales representative at 1-800-338-3987 or visit our Web site at www.mhhe.com/it.

# Visit www.mhhe.com/it
## THE ONLY SITE WITH ALL YOUR CIT AND MIS NEEDS.

# *Acknowledgments*

The Interactive Computing Series is a cooperative effort of many individuals, each contributing to an overall team effort. The Interactive Computing team is composed of instructional designers, writers, multimedia designers, graphic artists, and programmers. Our goal is to provide you and your instructor with the most powerful and enjoyable learning environment using both traditional text and new interactive multimedia techniques. Interactive Computing is tested rigorously in both CD and text formats prior to publication.

Our special thanks to Trisha O'Shea and Kyle Lewis, our Editors for computer applications and concepts. Both Trisha and Kyle have poured their enthusiasm into the project and inspired us all to work closely together. Kyle Thomes, our Developmental Editor, has provided superb feedback from the market and excellent advice on content. Jodi McPherson, marketing, has added her inimitable enthusiasm and market knowledge. Finally, Mike Junior, Vice-President and Editor-in-Chief, provided the unstinting support required for a project of this magnitude.

The Azimuth team members who contributed to the textbooks and CD-ROM multimedia program are:

Ken Rosenblatt (Textbooks Project Manager and Writer, Interactive Writer)
Raymond Wang (Interactive Project Manager)
Russell Polo (Programmer)
Michele Faranda (Textbook design and layout)
Jason Eiseman (Technical Writer)
Michael Domis (Technical Writer)
Larry Klein (Contributing Writer)
Thomas Grande (Editorial Assistant, layout)
Stefon Westry (Multimedia Designer)

# Contents

## PowerPoint 2000 Brief Edition

# Contents

## Continued

L E S S O N

# 1

# INTRODUCTION TO POWERPOINT

Microsoft PowerPoint is a computer application that helps you to create impressive and professional presentations. With PowerPoint, you can make on-screen presentations, overhead transparencies in both black and white and color, paper printouts, 35mm slides, or handouts that include notes and outlines of your presentation. You can even design a presentation to be placed on the World Wide Web. PowerPoint is an effective tool that enables you to easily organize and present information. Creating and editing text and graphics are made easy by PowerPoint's user-friendly features.

With PowerPoint you will be able to design a presentation using a premade template, or make your own starting from scratch. A quick and easy way to get started is to let PowerPoint aid you in designing a presentation by using a tool called the AutoContent Wizard. PowerPoint lets you add clip art, charts, clipart, photographs, video, and sound to further enhance your presentation. You can even publish a PowerPoint presentation on the World Wide Web where anyone with a Web browser can view it.

If you need advice or tips while using PowerPoint there is an extensive help facility built into the application, as well as the ability to access online support via the Web. PowerPoint has a feature called the Office Assistant that will offer guidance and tips, and answer questions. There is also an index that can be searched by keyword.

**CASE STUDY**
Trista Leven is a recent college graduate who was hired by a company that grows and installs sod in a variety of markets. The president of the company has asked Trista to use PowerPoint to prepare a short presentation to be used at an upcoming residential construction conference. Trista first needs to familiarize herself with the application. To do this, she will create a short presentation using the AutoContent Wizard, and use PowerPoint's many help features to obtain assistance.

# Starting PowerPoint

## Concept

To use PowerPoint, you must first start, or open, the application from your computer's desktop. The Windows 98 operating system permits you to open an application in a variety of ways. You can launch PowerPoint and other programs by using the Start menu, a Quick Launch icon on the taskbar, a desktop shortcut, or by finding the program's executable file through My Computer or Windows Explorer.

## Do It!

Trista wants to begin using and PowerPoint so she will launch the application from the Start menu.

1. Click the Start button ![Start] located on the Windows taskbar. The Windows Start menu will appear above the button.

2. Move the mouse pointer over Programs on the Start menu. The Programs submenu will appear.

3. Move the mouse pointer over Microsoft PowerPoint on the Programs submenu, as shown in **Figure 1-1**, and click the left mouse button. The PowerPoint application window will open with the PowerPoint dialog box displayed in the center of the window as shown in **Figure 1-2**. At this time you may also see the Office Assistant, a feature of the program that offers you help as you work. The PowerPoint dialog box contains four radio buttons that let you select one of four options for either creating or opening a presentation. There is also a list box that shows you PowerPoint files that have been opened recently. Since Trista is working with a fresh copy of the program, this box is empty and dimmed. At the bottom of the dialog box is a check box labeled Don't show this dialog box again that allows you to bypass the dialog box each time you start PowerPoint.

4. Your window may not appear exactly like the one shown here because PowerPoint can be installed in more than one way and the actions of previous user may affect the setup of your window. In the next Skill you will learn how to use the AutoContent Wizard to begin developing a presentation.

## More

The PowerPoint dialog box displays four options for working with a presentation. A presentation is a file composed of PowerPoint created slides. A slide is a single screen of your presentation. Using the AutoContent Wizard, PowerPoint's computer assisted presentation designer, is the simplest way to make a presentation and will be discussed in detail in the next skill. The Design Template option allows you to work with individual preformatted presentation designs. Blank Presentation is a feature that allows you to start from scratch (you will learn how to build an original presentation in Lesson 2). Finally, the Open an existing presentation option allows you to open a PowerPoint file that was saved previously.

Figure 1-1 Opening PowerPoint from the Start menu

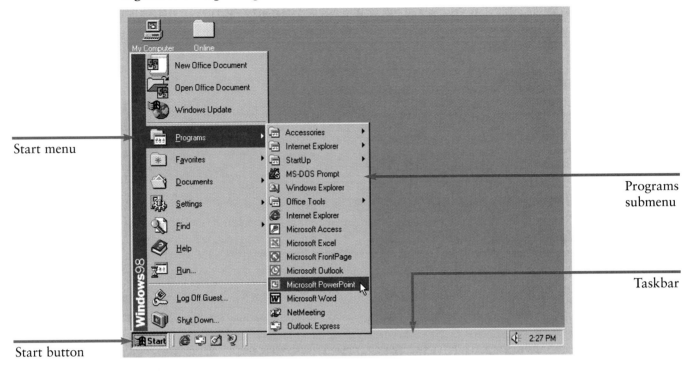

Start menu

Programs submenu

Taskbar

Start button

Figure 1-2 PowerPoint application window and dialog box

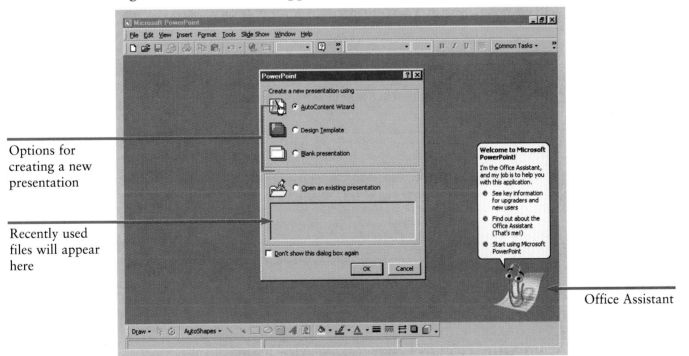

Options for creating a new presentation

Recently used files will appear here

Office Assistant

PowerPoint 2000

## Hot Tip

If the PowerPoint window does not fill the entire screen, you can click the **Maximize** button ☐ in the upper-right corner to expand the application window.

# Using the AutoContent Wizard

## Concept

The AutoContent Wizard is the easiest and quickest way to design a presentation in PowerPoint. It is a very useful tool for new users of PowerPoint and users who need to create presentations in a short amount of time. The AutoContent Wizard will assist you in basic layout design, style, and output type. All you have to do is add the content.

## Do It!

Trista wants to use the AutoContent Wizard to design a presentation.

1. Click the AutoContent Wizard radio button to select it, then click ⬚OK⬚. The AutoContent Wizard dialog box will open as shown in **Figure 1-3**.

2. Click ⬚?⬚ at the bottom of the dialog box to summon the Office Assistant if it is not already visible. The Office Assistant offers helpful tips as you work your way through PowerPoint, and will be discussed in detail later.

3. Move the pointer over the blue bullet labeled Help with this feature in the Assistant's balloon, then click the left mouse button. The Assistant will now provide you with descriptions of the AutoContent Wizard's steps as you advance.

4. Click ⬚Next >⬚ in the AutoContent Wizard dialog box. The second step of the AutoContent Wizard (**Figure 1-4**) will be displayed requesting that you select the type of presentation you are going to give. The presentation types are divided into categories. Currently, the General category is selected and its presentation types are listed in the box to the right of the category buttons.

5. Click the All button ⬚All⬚ to view all the presentation types at once. The first presentation type, Generic, should be selected by default.

6. Click ⬚Next >⬚. The next step of the Wizard asks you to choose what type of output your presentation will use.

7. Leave the On-screen presentation radio button selected and click ⬚Next >⬚. In the next step, Presentation options, you can add a title for your presentation and determine whether any information will appear in the footer, or bottom, of each presentation slide.

Figure 1-3  AutoContent Wizard

Outline tracks your progress through the Wizard

Click to summon Office Assistant

Click here for help with the AutoContent Wizard

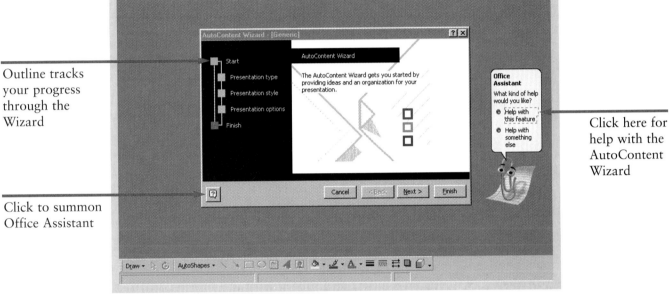

Figure 1-4  Selecting a presentation type

Presentation types in selected category

Click to return to previous step in Wizard

Click to advance to next step in Wizard

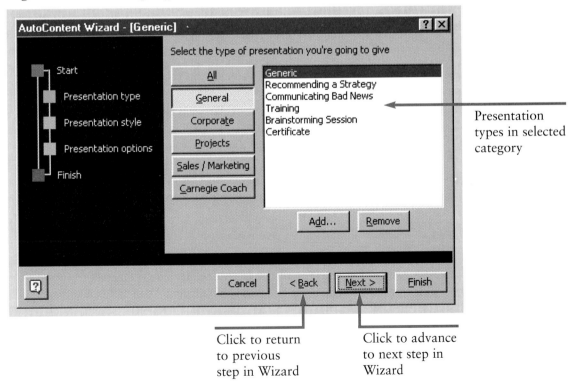

# Using the AutoContent Wizard (continued)

**Do It!**

**8** Move the pointer to the Presentation title text box (it will change to an I-beam when it is in the correct position), and click the mouse button. A flashing insertion point will appear in the text box. (If there is already information in any of these text boxes, delete it by dragging the I-beam over the text to select it and then pressing [Back Space], then replace it with the following text.)

**9** Type Learning PowerPoint as the title of the presentation.

**10** Press [Tab] to move the insertion point into the Footer text box.

**11** Type Trista Leven. Trista's name will now appear at the bottom of each slide. Below the Footer text box are two check boxes that allow you to include the date the presentation was last modified and the number of slides in the footer of each slide as well. Leave these boxes checked. The dialog box should resemble **Figure 1-5**.

**12** Click Next > . The Wizard informs you that it has enough information to complete your presentation. You may still return to any step of the Wizard to edit the content you have provided.

**13** Click the Finish button Finish . The Wizard dialog box closes and the presentation appears in the PowerPoint window in Normal view (see **Figure 1-6**). The AutoContent Wizard has created a number of slides, each with its own title and suggested discussion points. The first slide is displayed and includes Trista's name in the title. PowerPoint obtains information such as the user name during installation. You may also notice a wavy red line beneath Trista's name (or the name of the person to whom your copy of the software is registered). When PowerPoint's Check spelling as you type options is on, the program places these lines under words it does not recognize. These lines are nonprinting characters.

**More**

The PowerPoint AutoContent Wizard provides you with twenty of the most commonly used presentation types. The type you should choose depends on the message you are trying to convey. The AutoContent Wizard creates slides with text placeholders prompting you to insert pertinent information that will customize the presentation to fit your needs.

The Add button, located below the presentation type list, opens the Select Presentation Template dialog box from which you can choose additional presentation types. You may have to install these templates from your Office 2000 CD-ROM. You can also create your own presentation templates and make them available to the Wizard through this dialog box.

When creating a presentation with the AutoContent Wizard, you can click the Finish button at any time. The Wizard will complete the presentation with the information you have provided to that point.

Figure 1-5 Entering presentation options

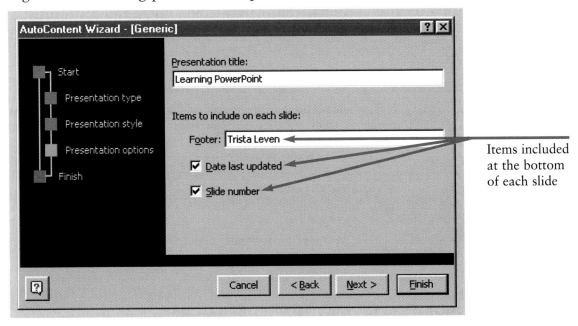

Items included at the bottom of each slide

Figure 1-6 AutoContent Wizard presentation in Normal view

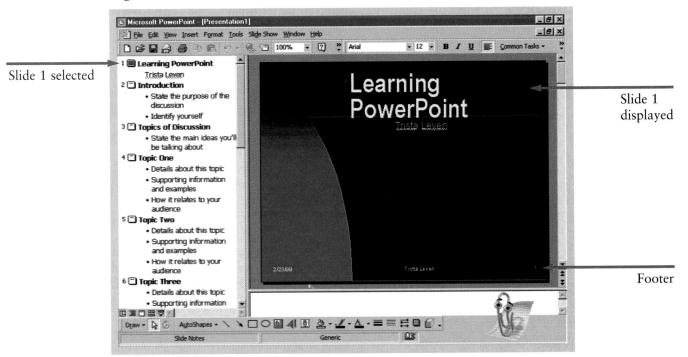

Slide 1 selected

Slide 1 displayed

Footer

PowerPoint 2000

The outline you see on the left side of the AutoContent Wizard dialog box is live. You can click on the square next to any Wizard step to go there immediately.

 **Exploring the PowerPoint Window**

**Concept**

Exploring a program's application window is an important step in learning to use the program successfully. PowerPoint's window is made up of several user-friendly features including toolbars, icons, and window viewing controls. PowerPoint is designed so that you can perform most of the program's functions from the main window. The application window is flexible and can be customized to suit an individual user's preferences.

**Do It!**

Trista will familiarize herself with the PowerPoint window to gain a better understanding of its functions and features.

**1** The presentation you created in the previous Skill should still be in the active window. Click the Slide View button 🔲 located in the row of five buttons at the bottom-left corner of the window. Your presentation will be displayed in Slide View with the title slide in the center of the window, as in **Figure 1-7**.

**2** At the top of the screen is the title bar, which shows the name of the application, PowerPoint, and the name of the active presentation. The title bar also contains three buttons: Minimize 🔲, either Restore 🔲 or Maximize 🔲, and Close ❌. Minimize reduces the window to a program button on the taskbar. Restore reverts the window to its original size and location. Maximize enlarges the window to fill the entire screen, and Close terminates the application. The Control menu icon 🔲, located on the left side of the title bar, opens the control menu which houses commands that are similar to the sizing buttons.

**3** Below the Title bar is the menu bar, which contains various menus of PowerPoint commands. Click File. The File menu will open below its menu title. When you move the pointer over a command on a menu, it will become highlighted. You perform operations in PowerPoint by clicking commands on a menu. Each menu consists of a list of related commands and has two levels. The first level appears as soon as you open the menu and contains the commands you use most often. If you do not choose a command, the menu will expand after a few seconds to reveal more options. The sizing buttons on the menu bar affect the file window and act independently of the application window's sizing buttons. For example, if you want to close the presentation you are viewing, but not the entire PowerPoint application, click the Close button on the menu bar.

**4** The row of icons and selection boxes below the menu bar contains two toolbars, the Standard toolbar and the Formatting toolbar. The buttons and boxes on toolbars serve as shortcuts to frequently used PowerPoint commands. The Drawing toolbar is currently active near the bottom of the window. To see a list of all toolbars available in PowerPoint, click View on the menu bar and highlight the Toolbars command. A submenu will appear with the names of all toolbars. A check will appear next to those that are currently active. Toolbars can be moved and resized, so your screen may differ slightly from the one you see on the next page. When you rest the mouse pointer over a toolbar button, a ScreenTip that identifies its function will appear.

**5** The main area of the screen is known as the presentation window. This is where you view and work on your presentation slides and their content.

*More*

The vertical and horizontal scroll bars allow you to view data that does not fit in the window. If the full height or width of a document does fit in the window, then the corresponding scroll bar will be inactive. There are various ways to use the scroll bars. Clicking on a scroll bar arrow moves the display in small increments. Clicking in the scroll bar above or below the scroll bar box advances the presentation one screen at a time. Dragging the scroll bar box allows you to scroll to any specific point in your presentation. In Slide View, clicking scroll arrows or in the scroll bar advances the presentation one slide at a time. Below the vertical scroll bar, the Previous Slide and Next Slide buttons serve this same purpose.

The status bar at the bottom of the window gives you feedback on your current activity in PowerPoint, including which slide you are viewing and the design template being used. If you double-click the current design name in the status bar, a dialog box will appear that allows you to choose a different design.

Figure 1-7  Presentation in Slide View

Title bar

Menu bar

Standard and Formatting toolbars

Sizing buttons

Scroll bar box

Vertical scroll bar

Scroll bar arrow

Presentation window

Horizontal scroll bar (inactive)

View buttons

Drawing toolbar

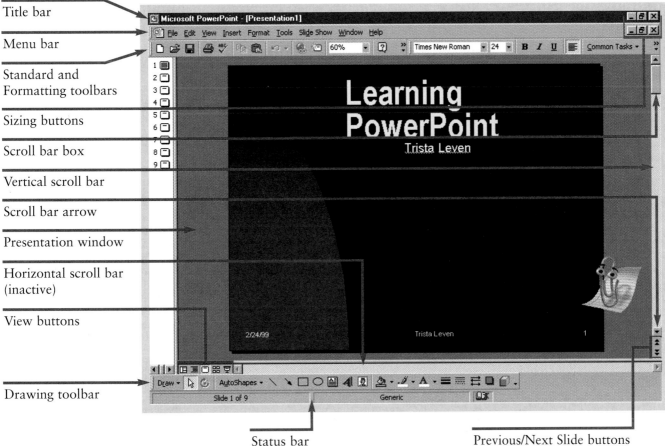

Status bar

Previous/Next Slide buttons

PowerPoint 2000

# Viewing Your Presentation

## Concept

PowerPoint offers several options for viewing your presentation. The different views allow you to focus on specific aspects of your presentation. The view you select will depend on the task you wish to accomplish, whether it be adding or editing text, adding graphics, organizing your slides, or previewing your presentation.

## Do It!

Trista wants to see how her presentation will appear in each of PowerPoint's views.

**1** The presentation is currently in Slide View. Slide View allows you to focus on one slide at a time. In this view you can add and modify your presentation's content, including text, graphics, and overall slide appearance. The list of numbered slide icons on the left side of the window offers you a quick way to display a different slide in the window. Simply click on the slide you want to view.

**2** Click the Outline View button. The presentation will switch to Outline View, as shown in **Figure 1-8**. This view displays the title and main topics of each slide in your presentation. It is best used for entering, editing, and arranging the text on your slides. Notice that like Normal View, Outline View has a three-pane structure. The outline occupies the large pane, while the right side of the window holds a thumbnail of the selected slide and a notes pane where you can type notes about the selected slide.

**3** Click the Slide Sorter View button. In Slide Sorter View, you can view thumbnails of all your presentation's slides at once in their proper order, as shown in **Figure 1-9**. This view is useful for rearranging slide order. It is also used for adding special effects and transitions to your slides.

**4** Click View, then click Notes Page. In Notes Page View, each slide is presented individually accompanied by a large text box (see **Figure 1-10**). This text box is provided so that you can add your own notes for each slide in the presentation that will not appear on the slides themselves. You can then print these notes and have them available when you give your presentation. You can also add notes to a slide in Normal View and Outline View.

**5** Click the Slide Show button. PowerPoint runs the presentation as a full screen slide show. Click the left mouse button to advance through each slide. When all the slides have been shown, you will be returned to the previous view.

**6** Click the Normal View button. Normal View is a three-pane hybrid of Outline, Slide, and Notes Page Views. Any changes you make in the outline pane will be reflected immediately in the slide pane, and vice-versa.

## More

PowerPoint's multiple views add significant depth to presentation design. Instead of being limited to one editing system you have a choice of several. In each view you also have the option to zoom in and out of the page. To access this option click the Zoom drop-down list arrow 40% on the Standard toolbar. Then select a zoom percentage. You are not limited to the percentage values in the drop-down list. You can click the Zoom text box to select the current zoom percentage, and then enter any value between 10 and 400.

Figure 1-8  Outline View

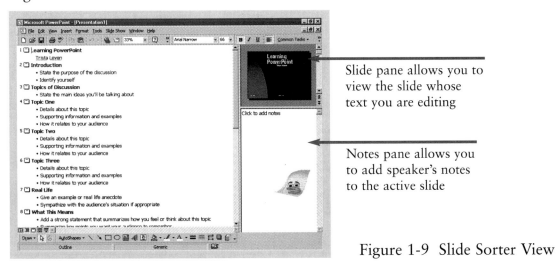

Slide pane allows you to view the slide whose text you are editing

Notes pane allows you to add speaker's notes to the active slide

Figure 1-9  Slide Sorter View

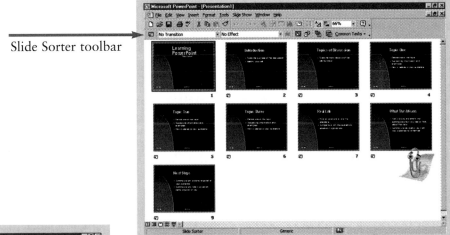

Slide Sorter toolbar

Figure 1-10  Notes Page View

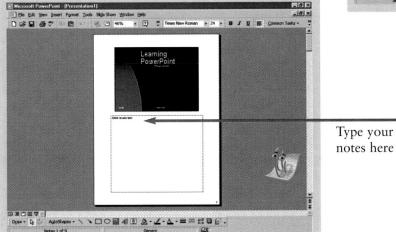

Type your speaker's notes here

PowerPoint 2000

*Practice*

Use the View commands and the Zoom control to examine the presentation in different views and at different magnifications.

*Hot Tip*

When using a view that has more than one pane, you can change the sizes of the panes to suit your needs. Place the mouse pointer over the border between any two panes, then click and drag the border to shrink one pane while expanding the other.

# Using the Office Assistant

## Concept

Even the most experienced computer users need help from time to time. The Office Assistant is a help feature that lets you ask questions related to your problems, and will reply with several help options that may be useful to you based on the question you asked. You can also configure the Office Assistant so that it senses your actions and offers relevant help tips as you work.

## Do It!

Trista has questions about designing a presentation with PowerPoint. She will use the Office Assistant to obtain answers to her questions.

1. Click the Office Assistant (if the Assistant is not visible, click Help, then click Show the Office Assistant first). The Assistant's dialog balloon will appear asking what you would like to do, and its text box will instruct you to type a question.

2. Type How can I design an effective presentation?

3. Click the Search button [ Search ]. The Office Assistant scans PowerPoint's Help files and returns the topics that are relevant to the question, as in Figure 1-11.

4. Click on the help topic titled Computer-based slide show design guidelines. A Microsoft PowerPoint Help window like the one in Figure 1-12 opens to display the help topic.

5. Read the topic, using the vertical scroll bar to bring the material that is not visible into view. Some help files, like this one, contain underlined blue text. These instances of text are hyperlinks that, when clicked, take you to related help files or other locations within the file you are reading.

6. Leave the Help window open.

## More

From time to time the Assistant will offer you tips on how to use PowerPoint more efficiently. The appearance of a small light bulb, either next to the Assistant or on the Microsoft PowerPoint Help button [?], indicates that there is a tip to be viewed. To see the tip, click the light bulb in whichever location it appears.

The Office Assistant can be customized. Click the [ Options ] button in its dialog balloon to open the Office Assistant dialog box. This dialog box has two tabs: Gallery and Options. The Gallery tab contains different assistant characters you can install, and scrolling through the characters provides you with a preview of each one. From the Options tab, shown in Figure 1-13, you can control the Assistant's behavior and capabilities, and decide what kinds of tips it will show. You can also access Office Assistant commands by right-clicking the Assistant itself.

Figure 1-11  Search results

Figure 1-12  PowerPoint Help file

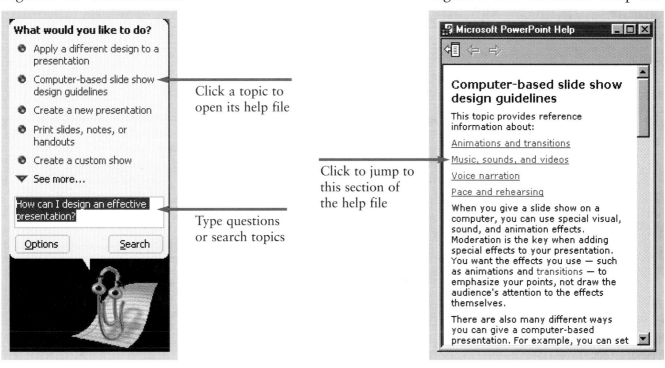

Figure 1-13  Office Assistant dialog box

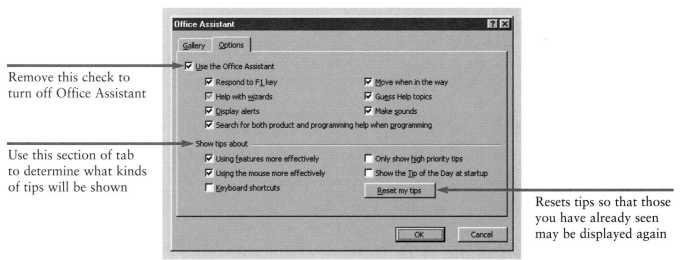

*Practice*

Use the Office Assistant's ability to answer questions to get help on the Office Assistant's options. When you are done, close any new Help windows that have been opened.

*Hot Tip*

The Office Assistant is common to all Office 2000 applications. Therefore, any Assistant options you change will affect it in all Office programs.

# Other PowerPoint Help Features

## Concept

Working with new software can be confusing, and, at times, even intimidating. Fortunately, Microsoft PowerPoint offers a number of built-in help features in addition to the Office Assistant. You can use these more traditional help features when you encounter problems or just have a question about a particular aspect of the program. This method of seeking help permits you to access all of PowerPoint's Help files instead of relying on the Office Assistant to find the correct ones

## Do It!

Trista will use PowerPoint's Help tabs to find out more about presentation slide output types.

**1** The Microsoft PowerPoint Help window you opened with the Office Assistant should still be on the screen. Click the Show button ◄▣ near the top of the window. The window expands to a two-paneled format. The left panel consists of three tabs that organize PowerPoint's Help files in three different ways. The right panel is used to display the actual Help files.

**2** Click the Index tab to bring it to the front if it is not already there. The Index presents PowerPoint's Help topics in an alphabetical list of keywords.

**3** Type output in the text-entry box labled 1. Type keywords. Notice that by the time you finish typing the word, the list box labeled 2. Or choose keywords has scrolled to match what you typed.

**4** Double-click output in the list box. All the Help topics associated with the keyword are displayed in the list box at the bottom of the tab, labeled 3. Choose a topic. The number of topics found is listed in parentheses.

**5** Click the topic titled Create handouts of slides (you may have to scroll down). The Help file is displayed in the right panel for you to read, as shown in **Figure 1-14**.

**6** Close the Help window. Then open the Help menu and click Hide the Office Assistant.

## More

The Index tab of the Help Topics dialog box is very helpful if you know what the task you are trying to accomplish is called, or if you know the name of the feature that you want to explore. If you are unsure of exactly what you are looking for, the Contents tab may be a better option for you. The Contents tab (see **Figure 1-15**) contains every Help topic that Excel offers, broken down by category, and is useful if you wish to obtain a broad view of the topics available. It is organized like an outline or the table of contents you might find in a book. It begins with general topics, symbolized by book icons, each of which can be expanded to reveal more specific and focused subtopics. Once you have revealed a general topic's subtopics, you can select a subtopic in the left panel to display it in the right panel, just as on the Index tab.

The **Answer Wizard** tab replicates the Office Assistant, allowing you to request help topics by entering questions or search topics in your own words.

Once you have clicked the Show button to display the Help tabs in a Help window, the button changes to the Hide button. Click the Hide button to collapse the window back to a single panel. The Help window also includes navigation buttons so you can browse back and forth among Help files you have already displayed. You can print a Help file by clicking the Print button 🖨 near the top of the window.

For quick help on a screen item or menu command, open the Help menu and click What's This? A question mark will be attached to the mouse pointer. When you click on the item in question with this pointer, a ScreenTip for the item will appear.

Figure 1-14 Using the Index tab

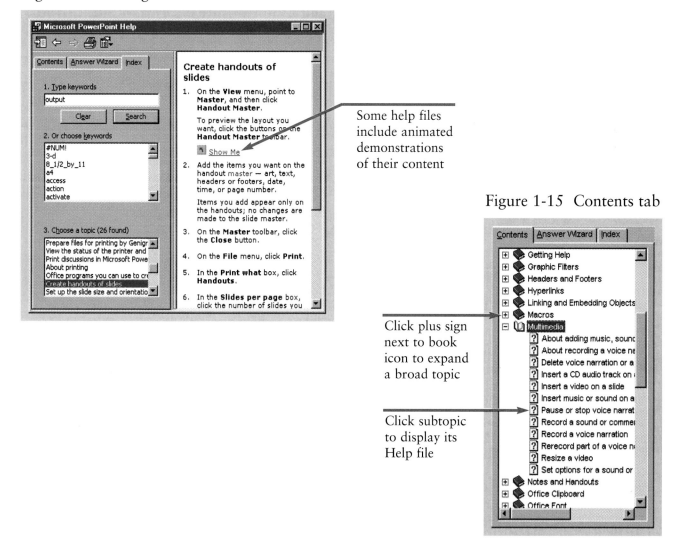

Some help files include animated demonstrations of their content

Figure 1-15 Contents tab

Click plus sign next to book icon to expand a broad topic

Click subtopic to display its Help file

PowerPoint 2000

*Practice*

Use the Index tab to get help on keyboard shortcuts, the Contents tab to get help on ways to get assistance while you work, and the What's This? command to get help on the Normal View button.

*Hot Tip*

To get help inside a dialog box, click ?. A question mark will be attached to the mouse pointer just like when you use the What's This? command.

# Saving and Closing a File

**Concept**

Saving your work properly is a crucial part of learning how to use application software. Once a file is saved, it can be reopened any time for viewing or editing. You can save your presentation to a hard drive, floppy disk, network drive, or even a Web server. Even after you save a file with a unique name, it is important to continue saving your changes to the file often. Otherwise, you could lose hours of hard work due to hardware, software, or power failures. Closing a file removes it from the screen and puts it away for later use. You can close a file while leaving the application open for use with other PowerPoint files. Or, if you are finished using PowerPoint, you can exit the application.

**Do It!**

Trista wants to save the presentation she created with the AutoContent Wizard in a new folder. Then she will close the file and exit PowerPoint.

1. Click File on the menu bar to open the File menu.

2. Click the Save As command. The Save As dialog box will open, as shown in **Figure 1-16**.

3. Click the drop-down arrow at the right edge of the Save in: box. A list of your available disk drives and folders will appear.

4. If you will be saving your files on a hard drive, click the drive labeled (C:). If your files are to be stored on a floppy disk, insert the disk and click the drive labeled 3½ Floppy (A:). Follow your instructor's directions if your files are to be stored elsewhere. The drive you select will appear in the Save in: box and its contents will be listed below in the contents window.

5. Click the Create New Folder button 🗋. The New Folder dialog box will open with an insertion point blinking in the Name: text box.

6. Type PowerPoint Files as the new folder's name (see **Figure 1-17**), then press [Enter]. A new folder named PowerPoint files has been created on the drive you chose earlier and selected in the Save in: box. The contents window is blank as the folder is empty.

Figure 1-16 Save As dialog box

Click to return
to the location
you selected
previously

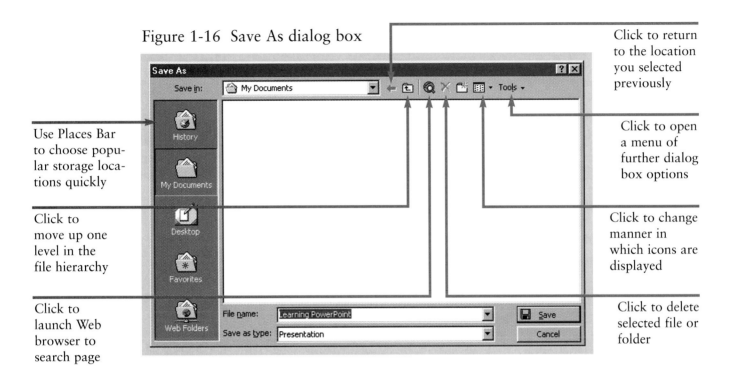

Use Places Bar
to choose popu-
lar storage loca-
tions quickly

Click to
move up one
level in the
file hierarchy

Click to
launch Web
browser to
search page

Click to open
a menu of
further dialog
box options

Click to change
manner in
which icons are
displayed

Click to delete
selected file or
folder

Figure 1-17 New Folder dialog box

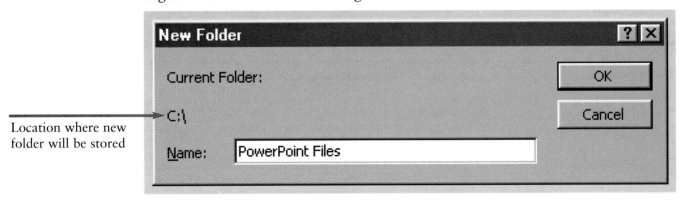

Location where new
folder will be stored

# Saving and Closing a File

## (continued)

### Do It!

**7** Now that you have chosen a storage location for your file, you must assign it a unique file name. The default name chosen by PowerPoint, **Learning PowerPoint**, should be highlighted in the **File name:** box. Depending on how your copy of Windows is configured, this name may be followed by the file extension .ppt. File extensions help an operating system associate certain file types with the appropriate applications. The extension .ppt identifies this file as a PowerPoint presentation file. You are not required to add the extension, as the program will do it for you.

**8** Type **My First Presentation.ppt** to replace the default file name.

**9** Click the Save button ⌹ Save . The file will be saved and you will be returned to the presentation window. Notice that the new file name now appears in the application window's title bar (**Figure 1-18**).

**10** To close the file, click File, then click Close, as shown in **Figure 1-19**. The file will disappear from the screen, leaving a blank, gray application window.

**11** To exit the application, click File, then click Exit. The PowerPoint application window closes.

### More

It is important to understand the distinction between Save and Save As commands. When you use the Save command you are telling the computer to make a copy of the current version of your file over the old version, deleting the previous copy. This is how you update a file so that includes the latest changes you have made. The Save As command allows you to change the name and/or the location of the file you are working on. This is useful if you wish to keep multiple copies of a work in progress without overwriting an older version. If you are saving a file for the first time, PowerPoint will open the Save As dialog box regardless of whether you choose Save or Save As so you can specify a name and location for the file. Once you have saved a file, you can save your changes quickly by clicking the Save button ⌹ on the Standard toolbar.

If you modify a file and do not save the changes before you close it, PowerPoint will ask you if you want to save the changes you have made. If you do not save, any modifications you have made to the file since the last time it was saved will be lost. PowerPoint will also prompt you to save changes if you try to exit the program with unsaved changes in a file.

Another important distinction to make is between the application and document close buttons ☒, which are identical. The document Close button is located on the right end of the menu bar, and is a shortcut to the Close command. Clicking simply closes the active presentation file. The application Close button is located on the right end or the title bar, and is a shortcut to the Exit command. Clicking this button closes down the PowerPoint application.

Figure 1-18  Saved PowerPoint file

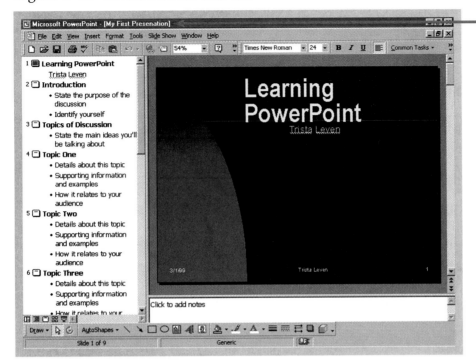

File name appears
in title bar once
file is saved

Figure 1-19  Closing a file

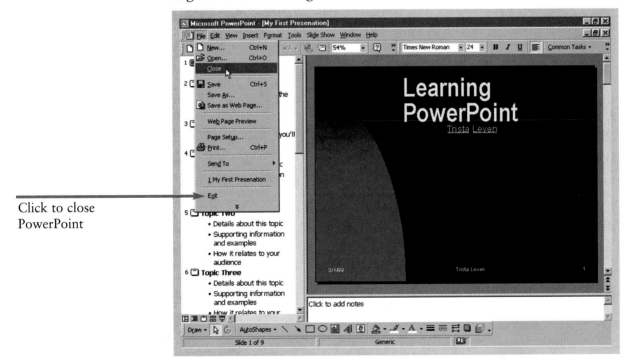

Click to close
PowerPoint

*Hot Tip*

The File menu contains a Save as Web Page command that allows you to save your presentation files coded in HTML (Hypertext Markup Language). Files saved in this manner can be published on the World Wide Web.

PowerPoint 2000

# Shortcuts

| Function | Button/Mouse | Menu | Keyboard |
|---|---|---|---|
| Office Assistant | 🔘 | Click Help, then Microsoft PowerPoint Help | [F1] |
| What's This? | | Click Help, then What's This? | [Shift]+[F1] |
| Close a file | ☒ | Click File, then click Close | [Ctrl]+[W] |
| Exit PowerPoint | ☒ | Click File, then click Exit | [Alt]+[F4] |
| Slide View | ▢ | | |
| Outline View | ▤ | | |
| Notes Page View | | Click View, then click Notes Page | |
| Slide Show | 🖵 | Click View, then click Slide Show | [F5] |
| Slide Sorter View | ⊞ | Click View, then click Slide Sorter | |
| Normal View | ▣ | Click View, then click Normal | |
| Save a file | 💾 | Click File, then click Save | [Ctrl]+[S] |

## Identify Key Features

Name the items indicated by callouts in **Figure 1-20**.

Figure 1-20  Features of the PowerPoint window

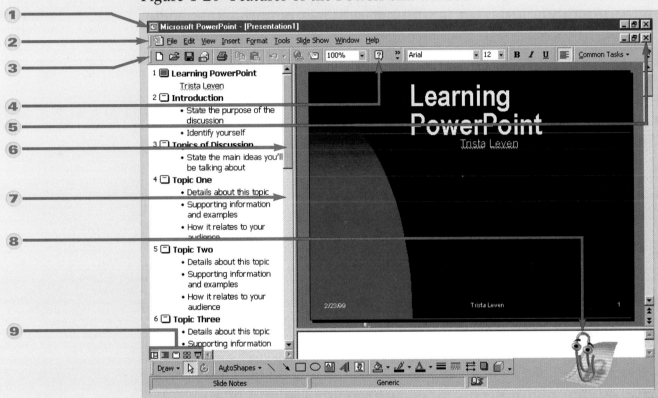

**PowerPoint 2000**

## Select The Best Answer

10. A quick and easy way to design a presentation in PowerPoint

11. Allows you to set options before executing a command

12. Useful for entering, editing, and organzing text on slides

13. Increases the size of the window so that it fills the screen

14. Organizes Help topics by broad categories and more specific subcategories

15. Allows you to focus on all aspects of one particular slide at a time

16. Help tab that functions like the Office Assistant

17. Permits you to choose a storage location and name for a file

a. Outline View

b. Answer Wizard tab

c. Save As dialog box

d. Contents tab

e. AutoContent Wizard

f. Maximize button

g. Slide View

h. Dialog box

## Complete the Statement

18. All of these are options for beginning a presentation except:

    a. AutoContent Wizard

    b. Open an existing presentation

    c. Design Template

    d. Finished presentation

19. To save changes to a file keeping its current name and location, click the:

    a. Save As button

    b. AutoContent Wizard

    c. Insert menu

    d. Save button

20. All of these are PowerPoint views except:

    a. Slide View

    b. 3-D View

    c. Outline View

    d. Slide Sorter View

21. Normal View consists of an outline pane, a slide pane, and a:

    a. Notes pane

    b. Slide Show pane

    c. Slide Sorter pane

    d. Help window

22. A wavy red line beneath text indicates a word that:

    a. Will appear on every slide

    b. Is part of the footer

    c. Is not recognized by PowerPoint

    d. Is a keyword

23. The best view for viewing all of your slides at once and rearranging their order is:

    a. Normal View

    b. Outline View

    c. Slide Sorter View

    d. Notes Page View

24. The toolbar at the bottom of the PowerPoint window is called the:

    a. Drawing toolbar

    b. Standard toolbar

    c. Formatting toolbar

    d. Index toolbar

25. The file extension for PowerPoint file is:

    a. .pow

    b. .doc

    c. .xls

    d. .ppt

26. If you wanted to obtain a ScreenTip for a screen item, you would use the Help menu's:

    a. Microsoft PowerPoint Help command

    b. Office Assistant command

    c. What's This? command

    d. ScreenTip dialog box

# *Interactivity*

## *Test Your Skills*

1. Start **PowerPoint** and run the AutoContent Wizard:

   a. Launch the PowerPoint application from the **Start** menu.

   b. Run the AutoContent Wizard from the PowerPoint dialog box.

   c. Do not use help from the Office Assistant.

2. Use the AutoContent Wizard to create a presentation:

   a. Choose the **Projects** category of presentations.

   b. Select **Reporting Progress or Status** as the presentation type.

   c. Select **On-screen presentation** as your output type.

   d. Give your presentation the title Test Your Skills 1.

   e. Include **your name** and the **slide number** in the footer, but not the **date last updated**.

   f. Click the **Finish** button to display the presentation.

3. View your presentation:

   a. Put your presentation in **Outline View**.

   b. Switch to **Slide View**. Use the **vertical scroll bar** to view each slide in the presentation in Slide View.

   c. Change to **Slide Sorter View**.

   d. Run a **Slide Show** of your presentation.

   e. Return the presentation to **Normal View**.

4. Use PowerPoint's Help facilities:

   a. Show the Office Assistant if not currently visible.

   b. Ask the Office Assistant about getting **help on the Web**.

   c. Select and read a topic provided by the Office Assistant that is related to your query.

   d. Activate the Help tabs.

   e. Use the **Contents** tab to located the same Help file you just read.

   f. Use the **Index** tab to list Help topics associated with the keyword **name**. Read the Help file titled **About naming presentations**.

   g. Close the Help window and hide the Office Assistant.

   h. Use the **What's This?** command to get a **ScreenTip** for the **Save as Web Page** command on the File menu.

**PowerPoint 2000**

# Interactivity (continued)

5. Save and close your presentation, then exit PowerPoint:

a. Save the presentation you created in your PowerPoint Files folder with the name TYS1.ppt.

b. Close the file TYS1.ppt.

c. Exit PowerPoint.

## Problem Solving

1. Tabak, Inc., a retail book distribution company, has recently expanded its operations to eight new cities across North America. It is important that the people staffing the new office are made to feel welcome working for the company. More importantly, they must be properly motivated for the expansion to be successful. You have been asked to lay the groundwork for a motivational presentation that employees at Tabak's remote sites can view over the Web. Use the AutoContent Wizard to create this motivational Web presentation, choosing the appopriate presentation and output types. The title of the presentation should be The Tabak Way, and the footer should include the phrase Beta version. Save the presentation as Solved1-1.ppt. Leave the presentation open.

2. Your colleague in the Corporate Services division of Tabak, Inc. has heard about the motivational Web presentation you are creating for employees at the company's new sites. The colleague thinks the presentation would be a valuable motivational tool for her department, even though most of the employees are not new. She would like to develop a similar presentation that is constructed specifically for the Corporate Services division. First, however, she wants to examine your work so that she can use it as a building block. Save a new version of Solved1-1.ppt as Solved1-2.ppt. Then close both presentation files.

3. Your boss has had bad experiences with losing large chunks of important data. He wants to be sure that PowerPoint has safeguards to prevent this from happening before he decides whether to adopt the software for the company. Use the Office Assistant to find out about how to recover lost presentations. When you find the appropriate help topic, print it so that you can present the information to your boss. Then, to demonstrate PowerPoint's user-friendliness, use the Index tab to locate the same help topic.

4. You have been hired as an Assistant to the Marketing Director at Redweb, an Internet service provider. In the coming months, you will be attending numerous trade shows in order to increase the company's profile. Use the AutoContent Wizard's Product/Services Overview presentation type to create a presentation that will attract attention to your company at these conferences. Give the presentation an exciting title and include appropriate information in the footer. Do not worry about the remaining content of the presentation, as you will learn how to add it later. Save the presentation as Solved1-4.ppt, and then exit PowerPoint. (Note: to create a new presentation when PowerPoint is already running, click File, then click New. The New Presentation dialog box will open to the General tab. Double-click AutoContent Wizard on the General tab to launch the Wizard.)

L E S S O N

2

# DESIGNING YOUR PRESENTATION

Presentation design is just as important as production. Choosing one style over another can make a big difference in how your presentation works. In PowerPoint you can design a presentation from scratch by choosing templates, colors and object placement.

PowerPoint makes designing a project from the beginning starting with a blank presentation easy to do. Slide AutoLayouts will help you organize the content of your presentation, and the design you select will depend on the data you wish to display. AutoLayouts are preformatted slides that contain placeholders for various objects, most useful of which are text boxes. It is in the text boxes that you will enter the information to be presented to your audience.

As you have learned, PowerPoint allows you to see your presentation in several different views. Using multiple views lets you work with your presentation most effectively. In Slide View you can focus on and manipulate every element of a single slide, while Outline View is a text-oriented display. To work with all of your slides at once, in the order that they appear in the presentation, you would use Slide Sorter View. Notes Page View lets you enter text that will not appear during your slide show but that can be referred to or distributed to your audience. Normal View is a tri-pane hybrid that allows you to accomplish several tasks without changing views. The appropriate view will depend on the task you need to preform.

**CASE STUDY**
In this lesson, Trista will design a presentation for the sod company that has hired her, Green Side Up, on her own from the beginning. She will start with a blank presentation, and use PowerPoint's design features to lay the groundwork for her project. She will also begin to add content to her presentation.

# Creating a New Presentation

**Concept**

PowerPoint allows you to create customized presentations from beginning to end. You can choose the style and layout of all features to give your presentation a personalized touch. Starting with a blank presentation gives you complete control over every aspect of the presentation's design. PowerPoint also gives you the option of beginning with Design Template, which can give you a head start in determining the overall organization and look of a particular project.

**Do It!**

Trista will create a presentation on her own, starting with a blank presentation.

1. Launch the PowerPoint application from the Start menu. When the application opens, the PowerPoint dialog box should appear.

2. Click the Blank presentation radio button, then click OK. The New Slide dialog box, shown in **Figure 2-1**, will appear over a blank presentation window. The New Slide dialog box offers numerous AutoLayouts slides. Each of these slides is set up differently to include places for text, pictures, and charts. The one you select will depend on how you want to present your information on a particular slide.

3. Click the slide icon named Table in the upper-right corner of the AutoLayout section. Notice that a border appears around it indicating its selection, and its name is shown in the area below the OK and Cancel buttons.

4. Click the Title Slide icon, then click OK. A blank title slide appears on the screen in Normal View.

5. Click File, then click Apply Design Template. The Apply Design Template dialog box opens, as shown in **Figure 2-2**.

6. Click the Design Template named Nature. A preview of the design will appear to the right of the list.

7. Click the Apply button Apply. The dialog box closes and the design is applied to the Title Slide, shown in **Figure 2-3**.

8. Save the file as GSU Presentation in your PowerPoint Files folder and close the file by selecting the Close command from the File menu. Do not close the application.

**More**

PowerPoint offers you other ways to create a new presentation. Clicking the New button on the Standard toolbar, or pressing [Ctrl]+[N] opens a new file and the New Slide dialog box. If you would like to browse all of the presentation style choices, click File and then select the New command. This will open the New Presentation dialog box from which you can choose a blank presentation, the AutoContent Wizard, a design template, or a specific presentation like those offered by the AutoContent Wizard. If you click the Common Tasks button Common Tasks on the Formatting toolbar, a menu will open with three frequently used commands: New Slide (adds a slide to your presentation), Slide Layout (allows you to change the AutoLayout for the current slide), and Apply Design Template.

Figure 2-1  New Slide dialog box

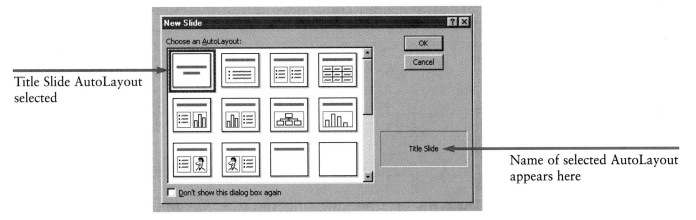

Title Slide AutoLayout
selected

Name of selected AutoLayout
appears here

Figure 2-2  Apply Design Template dialog box

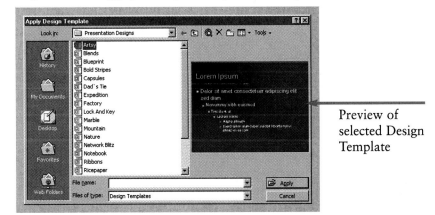

Preview of
selected Design
Template

Figure 2-3  Title Slide with Nature design

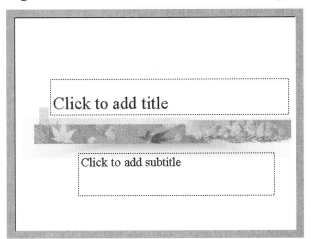

Click to add title

Click to add subtitle

**Practice**

Click the **New** button and create a **Title Only** slide. Its icon is the third one in the third row of the New Slide dialog box. Then apply the **Notebook** design template to this slide. Save your file as **MyPrac2-1**. Close the file when you are done.

**Hot Tip**

Right-clicking a blank area of a slide will open a pop-up shortcut menu from which you can choose the Slide Layout and Apply Design Template commands.

PowerPoint 2000

# Opening an Existing PowerPoint File

## Concept

To view or edit a file that is saved on a hard drive or floppy disk, you must first open it. The method that you use to open a file depends on whether PowerPoint is already running, your familiarity with the software, and your personal preferences.

## Do It!

Trista wants to open the GSU Presentation file she created.

1. Click File, then click the Open command. The Open dialog box will appear. The PowerPoint Files folder should be selected in the Look in: box. If not, click the drop-down arrow on the right end of the box to open a list of drives and folders available to your computer. Click the drive that contains your PowerPoint Files folder. Then, double-click the folder in the dialog box's contents window. Once the PowerPoint Files folder is selected in the Look in: box, the files it contains will be displayed in the contents window, as shown in **Figure 2-4**.

2. If it is not already selected (highlighted), click **GSU Presentation** to select it. A preview of the file will appear on the right side of the dialog box.

3. Click the Open button [Open]. The presentation will open on your screen in Normal View.

## More

If you have just opened PowerPoint and want to work with an existing file, click the radio button labeled Open an existing presentation in the PowerPoint dialog box. The list box below the button will become active (see **Figure 2-5**), allowing you to select a presentation from a list of recently used PowerPoint files. Click the name of the presentation you want to open, and then click the OK button.

PowerPoint provides a powerful search facility in the event that you cannot remember the name or location of a file. Click the Tools button in the Open dialog box and then choose the Find command on the menu that appears. The Find dialog box (see **Figure 2-6**) will open. From the Find dialog box, you can search any drive or folder accessible from your computer. You can conduct your search using a wide variety of properties including file name, the date the file was last modified, or even the name of the file's author. Each property has its own set of conditions that you can apply to the search. For example, the File name property allows you to find a file whose name includes, begins with, or ends with a specific character or combination of characters. You submit this value in the Value text-entry box. Use the selection and text-entry boxes at the bottom of the dialog box to set your criteria, and then click the Find Now button to initiate the search. If your search is successful, the file you requested will be selected in the Open dialog box.

The Open button in the Open dialog box includes an arrow on its right edge. Clicking this arrow opens a menu that provides commands for opening a file in a number of different ways. For example, the Open Read-Only command permits you to view a file, but prohibits you from saving changes to it. The Open Copy command creates a copy of the file you are opening and opens the copy instead. The Open in Browser command opens HTML files in your Web browser rather than in PowerPoint.

Figure 2-4  Open dialog box

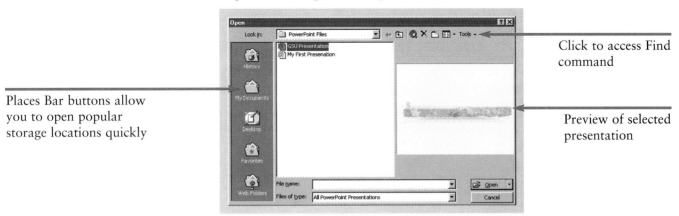

Click to access Find command

Places Bar buttons allow you to open popular storage locations quickly

Preview of selected presentation

Figure 2-5  Opening a file

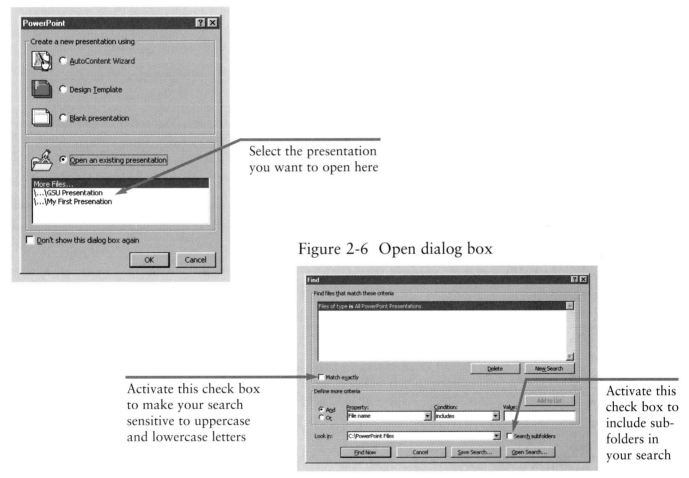

Select the presentation you want to open here

Figure 2-6  Open dialog box

Activate this check box to make your search sensitive to uppercase and lowercase letters

Activate this check box to include sub-folders in your search

**Practice**

Open the student file **Prac2-2**. Close the file when you are done, but be sure to leave Trista's presentation open for use in the next skill.

**Hot Tip**

Click the Views button in the Open dialog box to open a menu of choices for displaying the items in the contents window. The available Views are List, Properties, Details, and Preview.

# Entering Text in Normal View

### Concept

Text is an essential part of a presentation. It must be informative, organized effectively, and displayed appropriately. Entering text in Normal View allows you to see how it will look on the actual slide in the slide pane, while still allowing you to view it clearly and edit it in the outline pane. Many slides come with predetermined text placeholders containing instructions for their use. These text boxes are designated by dashed borders.

### Do It!

Trista will add text to her Title Slide using both the outline pane and the slide pane.

1. Click next to the dimmed slide icon ▦ labeled 1 in the outline pane (this icon represents the Title Slide). The icon will change to an active slide icon ☐ and a blinking insertion point will appear next to the icon.

2. Type the company name Green Side Up. Notice that as you type in the outline pane, the text also appears in the text box that contained the instruction Click to add title on the slide in the slide pane. The text on the slide is formatted with a font, font size, and color (see **Figure 2-7**) that are included in the Title Slide AutoLayout for the Nature Design Template.

3. Click the text box labeled Click to add subtitle to activate it on the slide in the slide pane. Type the company motto Merrily We Roll a Lawn, as shown in **Figure 2-8**. Then click a blank area of the slide to deselect the text box. Notice that the subtitle you just entered has its own set of formatting and it has also appeared below the slide title in the outline pane.

4. Click the Save 🖫 button to save the changes you have made.

### More

The outline pane and the slide pane in Normal View replicate the functions of Outline View and Slide View, respectively. For example, if you wanted to add text to a Title Slide in Slide View, you would click the Slide View button ▣, and then follow the same procedure that you used to enter the subtitle above. If you then switched to Outline View, you would see the new text that you added in Slide View.

Figure 2-7  Entering text in the outline pane

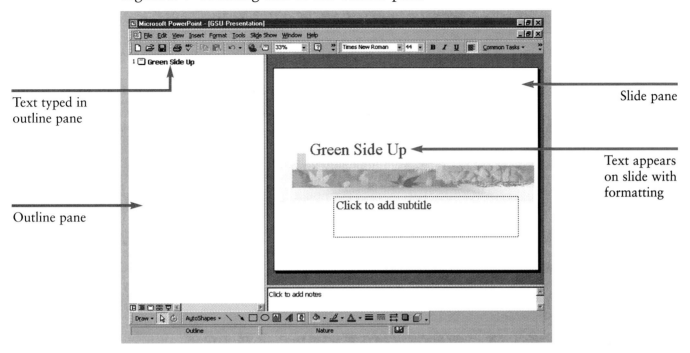

Text typed in
outline pane

Slide pane

Outline pane

Text appears
on slide with
formatting

Figure 2-8  Entering text in the slide pane

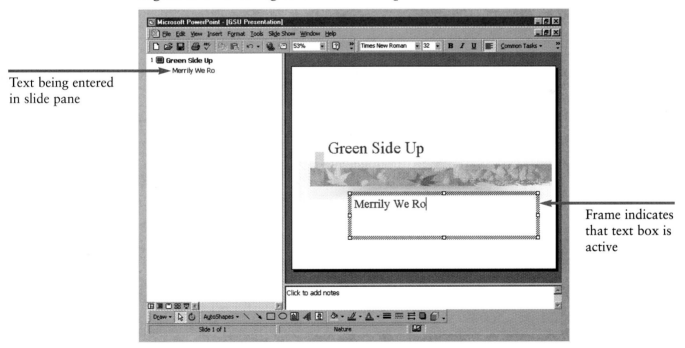

Text being entered
in slide pane

Frame indicates
that text box is
active

**Practice**

Open the file **MyPrac2-1**. In the title text
box, enter the name of a fictitious company. Save your file as **MyPrac2-3** when
you are done.

**Hot Tip**

If you want to reverse an action you have
performed because you have changed your
mind or made a mistake, click the Undo
button 🔲 on the Standard toolbar. Click
the arrow to see a list of your most recent
actions so you can undo several at once.

# Adding a New Slide to Your Presentation

### Concept

If you create your presentation without the help of the AutoContent Wizard, you will need to add each slide manually. Before adding a slide, you should have a clear idea of what kind of information it will contain and how that information will be presented. Once you have determined these factors, you can use one of several methods for adding a new slide to a presentation.

### Do It!

Trista has finished her Title Slide, and needs to add a second slide to her presentation.

1. Click the New Slide button 🔲 on the Standard toolbar. The New Slide dialog box will open.

2. Click the second slide icon in the top row, Bulleted List, then click ⬛ OK . A new slide will be created (see **Figure 2-9**) with the layout you just selected and the Design Template of the previous slide, Nature. The new slide is placed after the active slide (in this case after Slide 1) automatically. Notice that the status bar now indicates that the active slide is Slide 2 of 2.

3. In the slide pane, click the text box with the instruction Click to add title to activate it. Then type Growing to meet your needs as the title of Slide 2.

4. Click the text box labeled Click to add text to select it. Enter the following lines of text, pressing [Enter] after the first two entries:

   11.2 square miles of turf laid since company was founded in 1989
   4 varieties produced on 1217 acres
   Business has grown by an average of 21% annually

5. Notice that this text is aligned left and is displayed as a bulleted list. Click outside the slide's borders to deselect the text box. Your slide should resemble the one shown in **Figure 2-10**.

6. Click the document close button ⬛ to close the presentation. Save changes when prompted to do so.

### More

There are multiple ways to create a new slide for your presentation. The Insert menu contains a New Slide command that opens the New Slide dialog box. Pressing [Ctrl]+[M] is the keyboard equivalent of this command. In addition, you can click New Slide on the Common Tasks menu.

Holding down [Shift] while clicking the New Slide button will create a new slide with the same AutoLayout as the current slide.

Figure 2-9  New Bulleted List slide

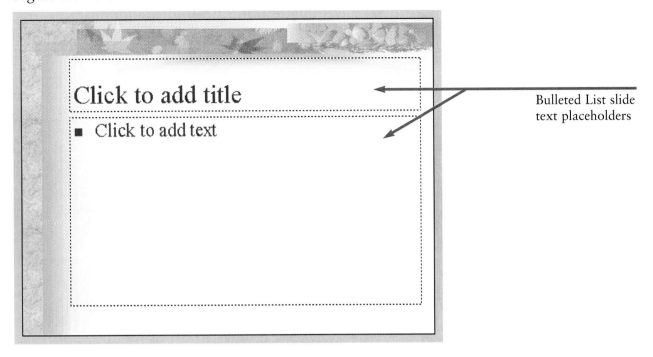

Bulleted List slide
text placeholders

Figure 2-10  Completed Bulleted List slide

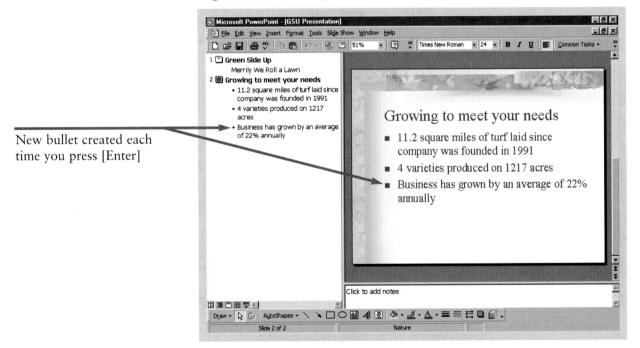

New bullet created each
time you press [Enter]

PowerPoint 2000

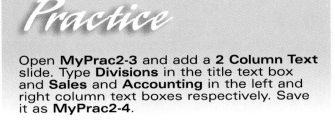

Open **MyPrac2-3** and add a **2 Column Text** slide. Type **Divisions** in the title text box and **Sales** and **Accounting** in the left and right column text boxes respectively. Save it as **MyPrac2-4**.

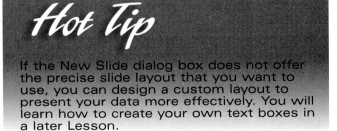

If the New Slide dialog box does not offer the precise slide layout that you want to use, you can design a custom layout to present your data more effectively. You will learn how to create your own text boxes in a later Lesson.

# Working with Text in Outline View

## Concept

PowerPoint allows you to view all of the text in your presentation at once in a simplified outline form. In Oultline View, text can be entered, edited, or moved about freely on newly created and existing slides. Text can also be moved or copied between different slides in the presentation. Outline View is also useful for promoting and demoting text, thereby increasing or decreasing its importance relative to the rest of the slide. While these tasks can also be accomplished in other Views, Outline View gives you more space to focus exclusively on your text.

## Do It!

Trista has added slides and information to her presentation. She wants to use Outline View to check the accuracy of her text and make any necessary changes.

**1** Open the student file Doit2-5, then save it to your Student Disk as GSU Presentation 2.

**2** Click the Outline View button ▣. The presentation switches to Outline View, as shown in **Figure 2-11**, showing the text of the slides that have been created in the outline pane and a thumbnail of the selected slide in the slide pane.

**3** Click the down arrow on the vertical scroll bar in the outline pane until the text for Slide 4 is visible in its entirety.

**4** Move the pointer to the left of the second-to-last bullet in the text of the fourth slide, Received the prestigious Velvet Turf award two years running, and, with the four-arrowed movement pointer ✛, click and hold.

**5** With the mouse button depressed, drag the line of text up to Slide 2, Growing to meet your needs, and position it at the bottom of the slide. As you drag the text, the pointer changes to a vertical double arrow ↕, and a solid horizontal line will appear. Make sure you do not drag horizontally first. The solid line shows you where the text will appear when you release the mouse button. Let go of the mouse button to drop the text into place (see **Figure 2-12**) at the end of Slide 2.

**6** Place the insertion point after the item labeled Playing Fields, the fifth bulleted item on Slide 4, by moving the mouse pointer there and clicking.

**7** Press [Enter] to create a new bullet, then type Commercial.

**8** Using the same technique that you used to move text between slides, drag the Corporate Parks bullet on Slide 4 down four places so that it comes directly after Commercial.

Figure 2-11  Presentation in Outline View

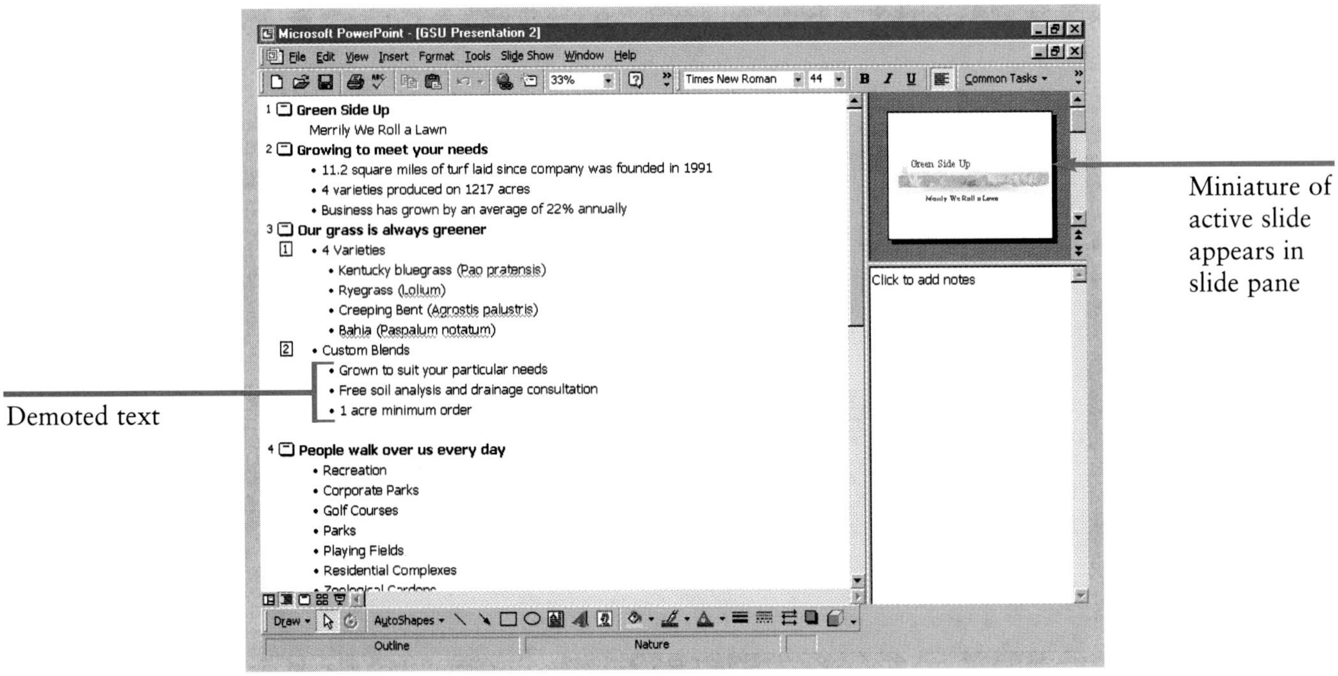

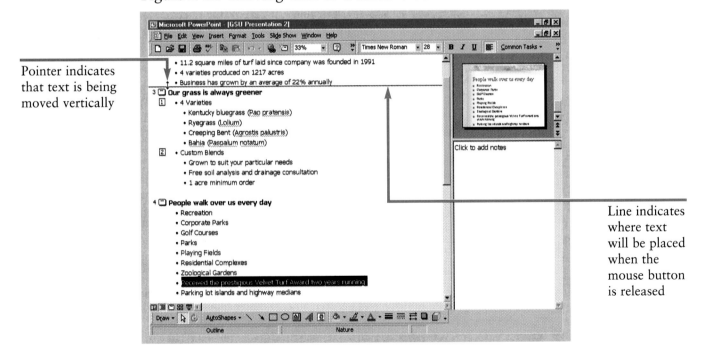

Miniature of active slide appears in slide pane

Demoted text

Figure 2-12  Moving Text in Outline View

Pointer indicates that text is being moved vertically

Line indicates where text will be placed when the mouse button is released

 Working with Text in Outline View (continued)

## Do It!

**9** Click View, highlight Toolbars, and then click Outlining on the submenu that opens. The Outlining toolbar will appear along the left side of the PowerPoint window.

**10** Click the bullet next to Golf Courses to select it. Then, hold [Shift] on the keyboard and click the bullet next to Playing Fields. This will add Playing Fields and all the items bwtween Playing Fields and Golf Courses to the selection.

**11** Click the Demote button ⬆ on the Outlining toolbar. The selected items are indented so as to be inferior to the heading above them, Recreation.

**12** Select the last five bulleted items on Slide 4 using the shift-click method you used earlier. Press [Tab] on the keyboard, which is equivalent to clicking ⬆, to demote these five items.

**13** Switch to Normal View. In the slide pane, click just to the left of the bullet labeled Commercial. This will activate the text box and select the bulleted item simultaneously.

**14** Click the Promote button ⬅ on the Outlining toolbar to move Commercial back to the same level of the outline as Recreation. Then switch back to Outline View. Your outline should resemble the one shown in **Figure 2-13**.

**15** Save the changes to your presentation.

## More

Pressing [Enter] in Outline View creates a new item at the same level as the current one. If you are at the top of the hierarchy, slide level, a new slide will be created. You can then press [Tab] or [Shift]+[Tab] where the insertion point is to demote or promote the current item. Promoting a second level item puts it on its own slide.

The Outlining toolbar provides buttons, shown in **Table 2-1**, that allow you to change the amount of information displayed with each slide. The Collapse All button reduces all of the slides to their titles only, hiding any other text. A grey line will appear under a title if there is any other text on that slide. The Expand All button can be used to view all of your presentation's text if any of the slides are collapsed. The Expand and Collapse buttons function in the same way as the Expand All and Collapse All buttons, respectively, but they act upon a single slide only. The Move Down and Move Up buttons relocate entire paragraphs or titles. Text that is moved up or down exchanges places with the next item in its path. The Demote and Promote buttons can be used to determine the level in the outline at which a particular item lies. Main points, aligned with the left margin, are at the highest level and each indentation to the right represents a drop in the outline's hierarchy. Similar items are grouped on the same level of an outline. Moving an item changes only its location, not its level. Changing an item's level with the mouse is the same as moving it by clicking buttons, but you must drag it horizontally first to get a different movement pointer ↔. A vertical line appears showing at what level the item will appear when the mouse button is released.

Figure 2-13  Rearranged outline

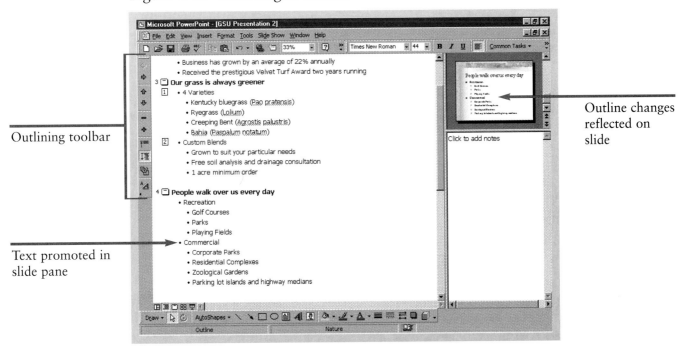

Outlining toolbar

Text promoted in
slide pane

Outline changes
reflected on
slide

Table 2-1  Outlining toolbar buttons

| BUTTON | NAME | FUNCTION |
|---|---|---|
| | Promote (Indent less) | Moves selected item to the left, or up one level |
| | Demote (Indent more) | Indents selected item to the right, or down one level |
| | Move Up | Moves the selection up in the outline by exchanging it with the previous item |
| | Move Down | Moves the selection down in the outline by exchanging it with the next item |
| | Collapse | Displays only the titles of selected slides |
| | Expand | Displays the titles and all of the bulleted items of selected slides |
| | Collapse All | Displays only the titles of all slides |
| | Expand All | Displays the titles and all of the bulleted items of all slides |
| | Summary Slide | Creates a new slide with a bulleted list of the titles of selected slides |
| | Show Formatting | When depressed, displays text with all its formatting, such as italics or font size; when deselected, all text appears identical on the screen to facilitate readability |

**Practice**

Open the file **MyPrac2-4** and switch to Outline View. Insert a new slide between the two existing slides. Title it **We Produce** and then create three bullets listing three services or products supplied by your company. Save your work as **MyPrac2-5**.

**Hot Tip**

Double-clicking a slide's icon in Outline View collapses or expands that slide's text, depending on its current state.

# Adding Speaker's Notes

---

### Concept

When giving a presentation, it is often helpful to have precise notes that refer to each slide in the order in which it will be shown. PowerPoint allows you to create notes pages which contain presentation notes along with a small picture of the slide being referenced. These notes do not show up as part of the presentation, but can be viewed privately or printed out for rehearsal and delivery. You can enter notes in Notes Page View or in the notes pane of any tri-pane view.

---

### Do It!

Trista wants to add notes to two of her slides so she can refer to them during her presentation.

1. GSU Presentation 2 should still be open in Outline View. Click anywhere in the slide title Our grass is always greener to make Slide 3 the active slide.

2. Click in the notes pane, which is currently blank except for the instruction Click to add notes. The instruction will be replaced by a blinking insertion point.

3. Type the following text, as shown in **Figure 2-14,** to accompany Slide 3:

   As you can see, we grow four types of grass to meet a wide variety of soil and light conditions. If these sods do not meet your needs, we can create a signature turf for a slight premium.

4. Click the Next Slide ⯆ button below the vertical scroll bar in the slide pane to advance to Slide 4.

5. Click View, then click Notes Page (when the View menu opens, you may have to wait a few seconds before the Notes Page command appears). In Notes Page View, the active slide is shown on a page with a text box in which you can enter notes for that slide.

6. Click the Zoom box drop-down list arrow `40% ▾`, then click 75%. The text box that appears beneath the slide will now be easier to read.

7. Click inside the text box (a Slide Miniature window will appear) to activate it and type the following text, as shown in **Figure 2-15:**

   We are experienced in handling both large and small jobs, laying sod on everything from exclusive 36 hole golf courses to parking lot islands measuring a mere three feet across.

8. Deselect the text box and save the changes to the presentation.

---

### More

The image of the slide that appears at the top of the page in Notes Page View is helpful when trying to coordinate your comments with your slides during the presentation. If you need more room for your notes, the size of the image may be reduced to allow extra room for additional text; this only affects this View and has no bearing on the actual size of the slide as it appears during the presentation.

Figure 2-14  Adding speaker's notes in the notes pane

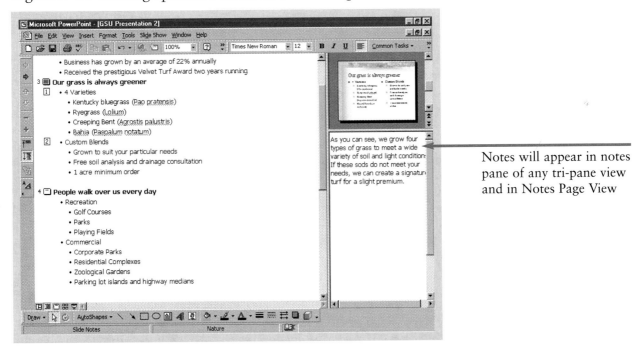

Notes will appear in notes pane of any tri-pane view and in Notes Page View

Figure 2-15  Notes Page View

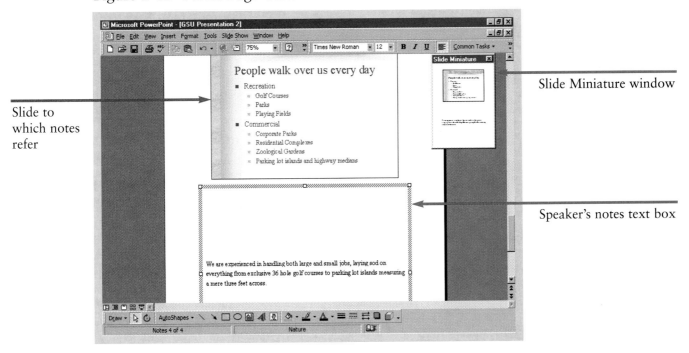

Slide to which notes refer

Slide Miniature window

Speaker's notes text box

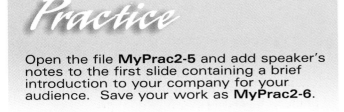

Open the file **MyPrac2-5** and add speaker's notes to the first slide containing a brief introduction to your company for your audience.  Save your work as **MyPrac2-6**.

*Hot Tip*

For making more complex notes which can be distributed to an audience, PowerPoint lets you export miniature images of your slides to a Microsoft Word page layout by clicking **File**, then selecting Microsoft Word from the **Send To** submenu.

# Printing Slides and Notes Pages

## Concept

You can use PowerPoint's Print features to produce speaker's notes, audience hand-outs, or a hard copy of your presentation. Printing a presentation can involve a single click of a button or setting numerous options to determine what elements of presentation are printed, and how they are printed. You can use this output to evaluate your own work or as part of your actual delivery. This Skill assumes that your computer is properly connected to a black and white printer.

## Do It!

Trista wants to print hard copies of her presentations's slides and notes pages.

1 Put the presentation in Normal View and select Slide 1.

2 Click File, then click Print. The Print dialog box, shown in **Figure 2-16**, opens.

3 Make sure that the Print range is set to All, that 1 copy has been selected in the Copies section of the dialog box, and that the Print what: box is set to Slides.

4 Click OK to print. Your printer will produce four pages, each displaying one slide from the presentation.

5 Open the Print dialog box. Click the drop-down arrow at the right edge of the Print what: box and select Notes Pages from the drop-down list (see **Figure 2-17**).

6 In the Print range section of the dialog box, click the Slides radio button, and then type 3-4 in the text box next to it.

7 Click OK to print the Notes Pages you created for Slides 3 and 4.

## More

The Print dialog box offers you many printing options. The upper portion of the dialog box, labeled Printer, allows you to select any of the printing devices to which your computer is properly connected. Clicking the Name box will open a drop-down list of printers, from which you can choose. As you have seen, the Print range area allows you to determine how much of your presentation will print. With the All option selected the entire presentation will be printed. Current Slide sends only the slide that appears in the window to the printer. Selection prints the slides that you have highlighted, and the Slides option lets you enter slide numbers so you can print nonconsecutive slides and ranges of slides. You can also instruct PowerPoint to print the slides in reverse order by stating a range in reverse, such as 12-1.

In the Copies section you can determine how many times each selected slide will print. Checking the Collate box tells the computer to print one copy of the full set of slides before starting to print the next copy. If this box is not checked, your document will not be collated by the printer. For example, if you were to print three copies of a presentation without checking the collate box, three copies of the first slide will be printed before the printer goes on to the second slide. If you know the Print dialog box settings are correct, click the Print button 🖨 on the Standard toolbar to bypass the dialog box and print immediately.

Figure 2-16  Print dialog box

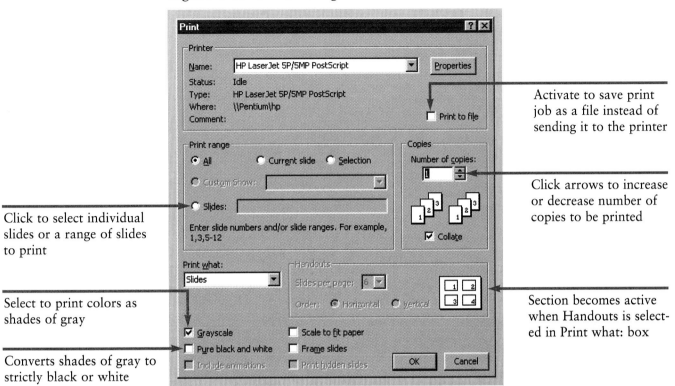

Activate to save print job as a file instead of sending it to the printer

Click arrows to increase or decrease number of copies to be printed

Click to select individual slides or a range of slides to print

Select to print colors as shades of gray

Converts shades of gray to strictly black or white

Section becomes active when Handouts is selected in Print what: box

Figure 2-17  Printing speaker's notes

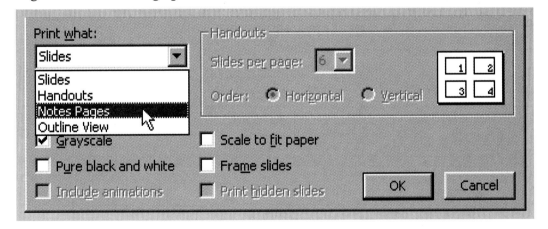

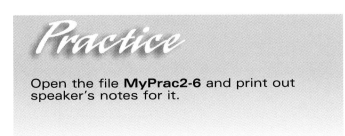

## Practice

Open the file **MyPrac2-6** and print out speaker's notes for it.

## Hot Tip

If you do not have a color printer, you can view your presentation as it will appear when printed in black and white by clicking the **Grayscale Preview** button on the Standard toolbar or by selecting the Black and White command from the View menu.

# Shortcuts

| Function | Button/Mouse | Menu | Keyboard |
|---|---|---|---|
| New file | ▢ | Click File, then click New | [Ctrl]+[N] |
| Apply Design Template | ▣ | Click Format or Common Tasks button, then click Apply Design Template | |
| New Slide | ▣ | Click Insert or Common Tasks button, then click New Slide | [Ctrl]+[M] |
| New Slide with same layout as previous slide | ▣ + [Shift] | Hold [Shift] while clicking New Slide command | [Ctrl]+[Shift]+[M] |
| Open a file | 📂 | Click File, then click Open | [Ctrl]+[O] |
| Promote selected text | ⬅ | | [Shift]+[Tab] or [Alt]+[Shift]+[Left] |
| Demote text | ➡ | | [Tab] or [Alt]+[Shift]+[Right] |
| Move text up | ⬆ | | [Alt]+[Shift]+[Up] |
| Move text down | ⬇ | | [Alt]+[Shift]+[Down] |
| Collapse slide text | ➖ | | [Alt]+[Shift]+[-] |
| Expand slide text | ➕ | | [Alt]+[Shift]+[+] |
| Collapse all slide text | ▤ | | [Alt]+[Shift]+[1] |
| Expand all slide text | ▤ | | [Alt]+[Shift]+[9] |
| Print | 🖨 To bypass Print dialog box | Click File, then click Print (opens Print dialog box) | [Ctrl]+[P] (opens Print dialog box) |

# Identify Key Features

Name the items indicated by callouts in **Figure 2-18**.

Figure 2-18  PowerPoint presentation in Outline View

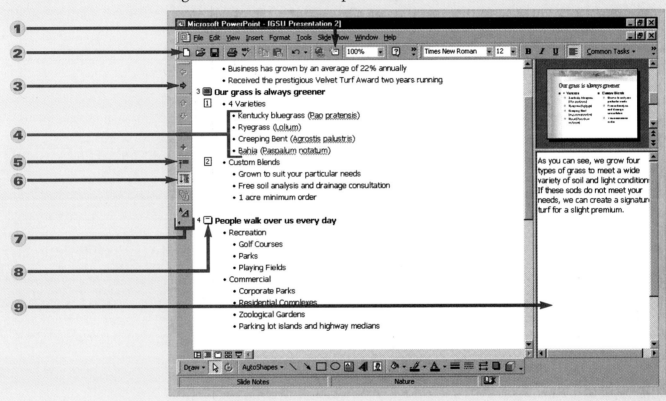

# Select The Best Answer

10. Displays all text of a selected slide or slides

11. Can show both collapsed and expanded slides

12. Allows you to choose an AutoLayout slide

13. Reverses the last action performed

14. Command that lets you choose an overall design for your presentation

15. Opens a menu of frequently used commands

16. Includes a search facility for locating files

17. An example of an AutoLayout slide

18. Allows you to determine which slides will printed

a. Undo command

b. New Slide dialog box

c. Open dialog box

d. Expand button

e. Outline View

f. Bulleted List

g. Print range

h. Apply Design Template

i. Common Tasks button

# Complete the Statement

19. You can insert a new slide by doing any of the following except:

   a. Clicking the New Slide button

   b. Using the Outlining toolbar

   c. Pressing [Control]+[M]

   d. Pressing [Enter] at the top level in Outline View

20. The Print dialog box allows you to print all of the following items individually except:

   a. Handouts

   b. Slides

   c. Footers

   d. Notes Pages

21. Notes that you enter in the notes pane can also be viewed:

   a. In the outline pane

   b. On the slide itself

   c. As part of the slide show

   d. In Notes Page View

22. To work more effectively in Outline View, you should activate:

   a. Grayscale Preview mode

   b. The Outlining toolbar

   c. The Drawing toolbar

   d. ScreenTips

23. Text that you place on presentation slides is contained in:

   a. Icons

   b. External files

   c. Text boxes

   d. AutoLayout slides

24. A tri-pane window is available in both Normal View and:

   a. Black and White View

   b. Notes Page View

   c. Slide Sorter View

   d. Outline View

25. To change the AutoLayout of a slide you have already created, select it and choose the:

   a. Slide Layout command

   b. New Slide command

   c. AutoContent Wizard

   d. Apply Design Template command

26. You can access the AutoContent Wizard, a blank presentation, or Design Templates from the:

   a. Slide pane

   b. Outline pane

   c. New Slide dialog box

   d. New Presentation dialog box

# Interactivity

## Test Your Skills

1. Design a presentation about your favorite musicians from scratch:

   a. Start PowerPoint.

   b. Select **Blank presentation**.

   c. Make your first slide a **Title Only** slide.

   d. Apply the Design Template **Marble** to your presentation.

   e. Enter the title **My Top 5 Musical Acts** on Slide 1.

2. Develop your presentation:

   a. Add five **Bulleted List** slides to your presentation, maintaining the Marble design.

   b. Switch to **Slide View**.

   c. Use the text box provided by the Bulleted List AutoLayout to title each of Slides 2 and 3 with the name of a favorite musical act.

   d. Switch to **Normal View**.

   e. Use the slide pane to title each of Slides 4 and 5 with the name of a favorite musical act.

   f. Use the outline pane to title Slide 6 with the name of a favorite musical act.

3. Focus on your presentation's text:

   a. Switch to **Outline View**.

   b. On Slides 2-6, add a line below the slide title that says **Favorite Albums**.

   c. List your three favorite albums for each musical act on the appropriate slide, demoted one level below Favorite Albums.

   d. Add a line on Slides 2-6 that says **Favorite Songs** on the same level as the Favorite Albums bullet.

   e. List your three favorite songs for each musical act on the appropriate slide, demoted one level below the Favorite Songs bullet.

   f. Move the Favorite Albums section of text so that it follows the Favorite Songs section on each slide (2-6).

   g. Collapse Slides 1 and 2.

   h. Collapse all of the remaining slides.

4. Create speaker's notes for your presentation:

   a. Use the **notes pane** in Outline View to write an introduction to your presentation that will accompany Slide 1.

   b. Switch to Notes Page View.

   c. Add notes to Slides 2-6 that include any biographical information you know about each musical act and why you enjoy their music.

# Interactivity (continued)

5. Create output for your presentation:

   a. Put your presentation in Normal View on Slide 1.

   b. Preview the presentation in black and white.

   c. Print a copy of each of your slides.

   d. Print your Notes Pages.

---

## Problem Solving

1. In Lesson 1, you were asked to lay the groundwork for a motivational presentation to be used by employees at the new offices of Tabak, Inc., a retail book distributor. Now that you have started to develop your PowerPoint skills, you can begin to convert the presentation you created from a framework into a functional, customized document. Open the file you created at the end of Lesson 1, Solved1-1.ppt. Since you produced this presentation with the AutoContent Wizard, each slide contains placeholder text that serves as a guide for what information should be included. Replace these placeholders with text that is relevant to Tabak and the goals of the presentation. Add Notes Pages for at least half of the slides, including the first and last slides. Save the presentation as Solved2-1.ppt.

2. In your search for a new job, you have encountered an employment agent who encourages you to present yourself as being highly skilled in application software. Along those lines, she has suggested that you use PowerPoint to create an interactive resume. Your resume should include at least seven slides, beginning with a Title Slide that provides personal information such as your name, address, and telephone number. Each of the slides that follows should cover a standard resume heading such as objective, education, experience, skills, etc. Choose a Design Template that you like, but that is also appropriate for the purpose of the presentation. When you finish the presentation, preview it in black and white, and the print out your slides. Save the project as Solved2-Resume.ppt.

3. Create a presentation that will allow you to chart your progress as you learn PowerPoint. Include a Title Slide for each Lesson in this book. Each Title Slide should be followed by individual slides for each Skill covered in that Lesson. Of course, for now you need only build the presentation through Lesson 2. Save the file as Solved2-3.ppt.

4. The Marketing Director at Redweb has approved the presentation layout that you submitted. With the first round of trade shows just a few weeks away, it is time to start developing a presentation that will attract potential clients to your company's Internet service. Open the Product/Services Overview presentation you created with the AutoContent Wizard at the end of Lesson 1 (Solved1-4.ppt). Using the placeholder text as a guide, add your own text to the presentation to make it a powerful marketing tool for Redweb. Add speaker's notes that detail exactly what the presenter should say as each slide is shown. Print your Notes Pages so you can submit them to your boss for approval. Save the new version of the presentation as Solved2-4.ppt.

L E S S O N

# 3

........................................................

# DEVELOPING YOUR PRESENTATION

........................................................

During the presentation building process you will invariably need to add, edit, and format text. PowerPoint comes equipped with an extensive collection of tools that can be used to manipulate text and text boxes. The ability to add your own text boxes at any location on a slide adds flexibility to your presentation designs. You are not limited to the preformatted and prepositioned text boxes provided by the AutoLayout slides. The placement of text on a slide can help you to accentuate the point you are making. Text boxes can be moved to any position on a slide with a simple drag of the mouse.

Editing text includes revising existing text, correcting typos, rearranging text, and checking and correcting misspellings. PowerPoint handles text much like the word processors you may have used. You can specify what font you wish your text to be in and add formatting. Text embellishments such as bolding and italics make text stand out. With PowerPoint's advanced editing tools you can check your spelling, and quickly search for and replace specific words or phrases. Each of these editing features will aid you in creating an impressive, grammatically correct presentation.

Once you have conquered the text of your presentation, you may want to enhance the presentation visually by adding drawing objects. Drawing objects can serve a functional purpose or simply be decorative.

**CASE STUDY**
Trista will develop her presentation by editing her existing text and adding her own custom text boxes. She will then use PowerPoint's editing tools to refine her text. Finally, she will enhance the appearance of the presentation by using PowerPoint's Drawing toolbar.

# Editing and Adding Text Boxes

**Concept**

Text in a PowerPoint presentation appears in text boxes. You can edit text in a text box, and add new text boxes anywhere on a slide. You can create two types of text boxes with the Text Box tool: text label and word processing. In a text label box, words do not wrap to the next line when they reach the edge of the text box. This type of box is best used for single words and short phrases. If you have a longer passage of text and want it to wrap to the next line at the edge of the box, then you should create a word processing box.

**Do It!**

Trista has added a fifth slide to her presentation and wants to edit some of the text on it. She will then add another slide and create her own text boxes on it.

1 Open the file Doit3-1, and save it as GSU Presentation 3.

2 Advance the presentation to Slide 5, which is a 2 Column Text slide that compares Green Side Up to its competition. Notices that the slide title, We Mow Down the Competition, uses uppercase letters throughout whereas the previous slide titles only use an uppercase letter for the first word.

3 Move the mouse pointer over the title text. The pointer will change from the standard pointing arrow to an I-beam I. Position the I-beam just after the M in Mow and click the left mouse button. A hashed border will appear around the text defining the box's dimensions and indicating that it is active. A flashing insertion point will also appear where you clicked to mark the place where entered text will be inserted or deleted.

4 Press [Back Space] to delete the upper case M, then type a lowercase m.

5 Press the right arrow key until the insertion point is just in front of the D in Down.

6 Press [Delete], which erases the character directly in front of the insertion point, and type a lowercase d.

7 Using the mouse, click and drag over the C in Competition to select it. Then type a lowercase c to replace it. The slide should now resemble **Figure 3-1**.

8 Press [Ctrl]+[M] (shortcut to the New Slide command) to open the New Slide dialog box. Select the Blank AutoLayout and click ⬚ OK ⬚ to add it as Slide 6.

9 Click 🖳 to switch to Slide View.

10 Click the **Text Box** button 📧 on the Drawing toolbar (if you do not see the Drawing toolbar, activate it from the View menu). The mouse pointer will now appear as a text cursor ↓ when it is in the document window. The position of the pointer on the slide determines where a text box will be created when the mouse button is clicked.

11 Move the mouse pointer to the upper-left corner of the blank part of the slide and click once. An active text label text box will appear, as shown in **Figure 3-2**.

Figure 3-1 Editing text

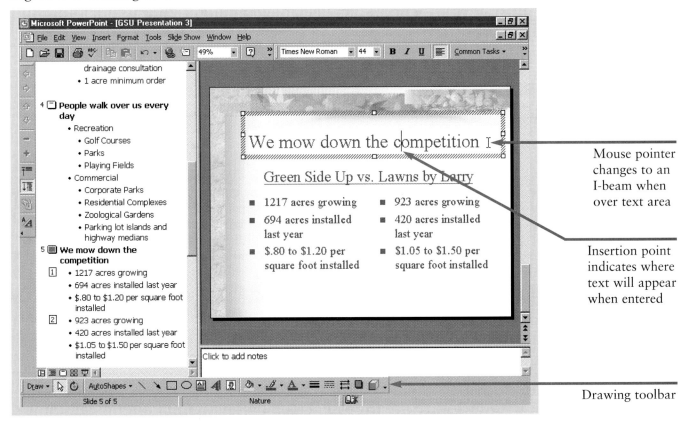

Mouse pointer changes to an I-beam when over text area

Insertion point indicates where text will appear when entered

Drawing toolbar

Figure 3-2 Creating a text label text box

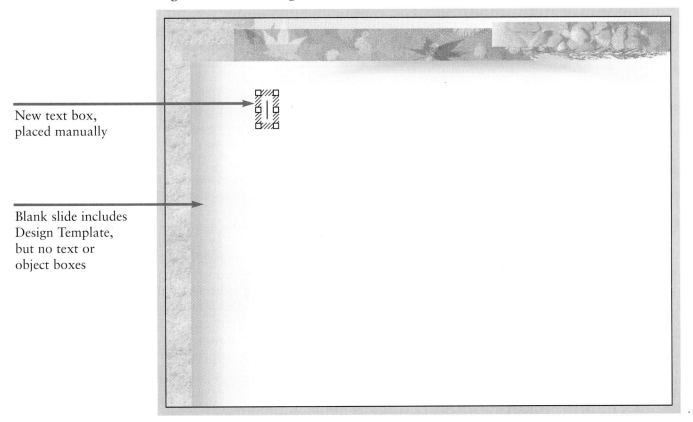

New text box, placed manually

Blank slide includes Design Template, but no text or object boxes

# Editing and Adding Text Boxes (continued)

## Do It!

**12** Type We're on a roll. The text box extends as you type to accommodate the text.

**13** Click the Text Box button 🖳 again.

**14** Position the text cursor below the left side of the text label box you created. Then click and drag from that point down to the bottom-right corner of the slide. As you drag, the text cursor will change to a drag pointer +, and a dashed border will indicate the dimensions of the box you are creating. When you release the mouse button, the box will retain its width, but its height will be reduced to one line. The height will be determined by the amount and size of text that you enter.

**15** Enter the following text (include misspellings, which you will learn how to correct later in this lesson):

> Argyle County Municiple Stadium (press [Enter])
> Winter Crow Golf Course and Country Club (press [Enter])
> Arthur B. Milton Golden Cloud Seniors Palace, Infirmary
> Care, and Recreational Facility

You may have noticed that the last line wrapped (see **Figure 3-3**), or continued on the next line, when it reached the boundary of the text box. The word processing text box that you created by dragging the text cursor allows this feature. A text label box will not wrap, but will continue on the same line until [Enter] is pressed.

**16** Create a text label box on the right half of the bottom of the slide.

**17** Type Recently Acquired Accounts.

**18** Click outside of the text box to deselect it. The slide should now approximately resemble the one shown in **Figure 3-4**.

**19** Save the changes you have made.

## More

The drag-and-drop method of copying and moving text is a convenient way to rearrange text in your slides. To move a section of text that you have selected, click it and drag the mouse pointer. When it is dragged, the mouse pointer will appear with a small box 🖑 indicating that text is loaded and is ready to be dropped. A dotted insertion point │ moves through the text with the drag-and-drop pointer, indicating where the loaded text will be dropped when you release the mouse button. If you wish to duplicate existing text elsewhere on a slide, it can be copied in a similar fashion by pressing [Ctrl] before the text is dropped. The drag-and-drop pointer will be tagged with a plus sign 🖑, notifying you that when the text is dropped into place, the original will be left untouched.

Figure 3-3  Word processing text box

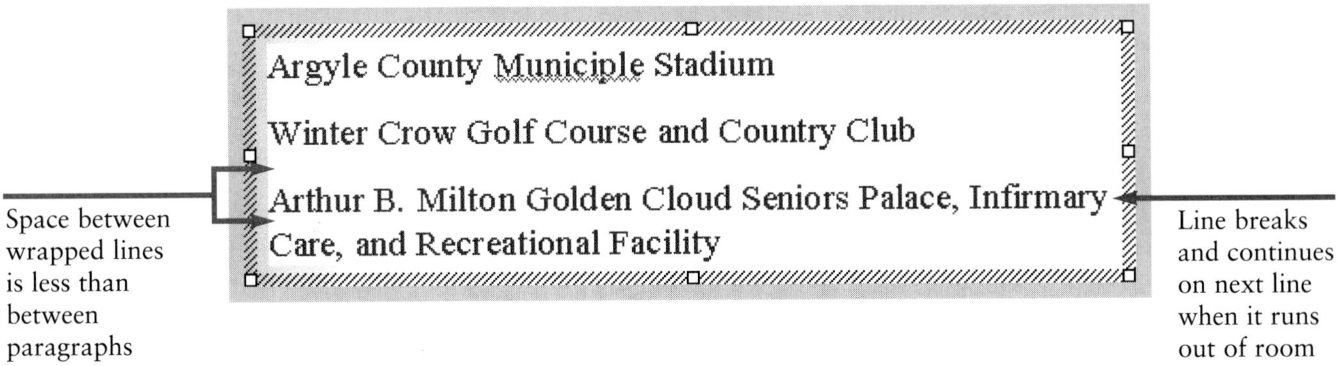

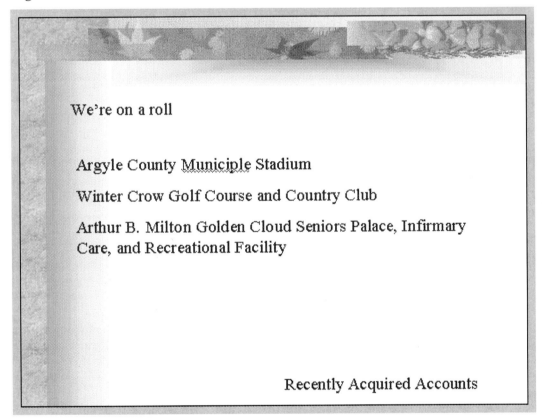

Space between wrapped lines is less than between paragraphs

Line breaks and continues on next line when it runs out of room

Figure 3-4  Slide with various text boxes added

Open the File **MyPrac2-6** and add a blank slide to the end of the presentation. Create a text label box in the upper-left corner that says **Board of Directors**, and a main text box in the body of the slide with three names in it. Save the file as **MyPrac3-1**.

To position items on a slide more accurately, you can display horizontal and vertical rulers by right-clicking a blank area of the slide and selecting Ruler from the pop-up menu that appears.

# Formatting Text

## Concept

Most of the text you have added to your presentation so far has appeared with certain preassigned characteristics known collectively as **formatting**. Formatting includes the overall appearance of the text, which is determined by the **font** that has been applied to it. Formatting also includes **font size**, **font color**, and **style**. PowerPoint gives you the ability to format text as you please, even if it was preformatted as part of a Design Template. Formatting can be applied for informational, organizational, and stylistic purposes.

## Do It!

Trista wants to change the formatting of the text on the last slide she created.

**1** If your Standard and Formatting toolbars currently occupy the same row in the PowerPoint window, place the mouse pointer over the left edge of the Formatting toolbar so that the pointer changes to a four-headed movement pointer ✛. Click and drag the Formatting toolbar down and to the left so that it rests directly below the Standard toolbar in its own row. The full Formatting toolbar will be visible, as shown in **Figure 3-5**.

**2** Click the text **We're on a Roll** on Slide 6 to activate the text box.

**3** Click at one end of the text box and drag the I-beam across the text to the other end to select the whole title.

**4** Click the drop-down list arrow on the right end of the **Font Size** box 24 ▾. The Font Size drop-down list will appear with the current font size highlighted.

**5** Scroll down the list and click **44**. The point size of the title text will increase. Points are the measurement unit used for character size and are equal to ½ of an inch.

**6** Click the **Font Color** drop-down list arrow 🅰▾ on the Drawing toolbar. The Font Color palette (shown in **Figure 3-6**) will appear, with a depressed button indicating the current color.

**7** Click the dark blue box, fourth from the left in the row of colored boxes (when you point to it a ScreenTip saying **Follow Title Text Scheme Color** should appear). The color palette will disappear and the color of the slide title will be changed.

**8** Click the **Italic** button *I*. The text will be italicized.

**9** Click the **Text Shadow** button ⑧. A shadow will be added behind the title. Click anywhere outside of the text box to deselect it and view the formatting changes. The title text should resemble **Figure 3-7**.

**10** Click the list of new accounts to activate their text box, and then select the three account names by dragging the I-beam from the beginning of the first line to the end of the last.

**11** Click the **Font** drop-down list arrow Times New Roman ▾ on the Standard toolbar . A list of fonts installed on your computer will appear.

Figure 3-5 Formatting toolbar

Text alignment buttons

Increase or Decrease Font Size

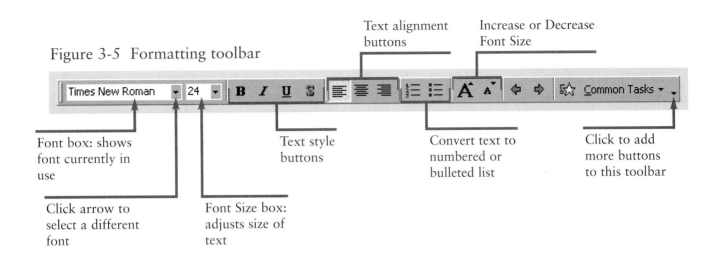

Font box: shows font currently in use

Text style buttons

Convert text to numbered or bulleted list

Click to add more buttons to this toolbar

Click arrow to select a different font

Font Size box: adjusts size of text

Figure 3-6 Font Color palette

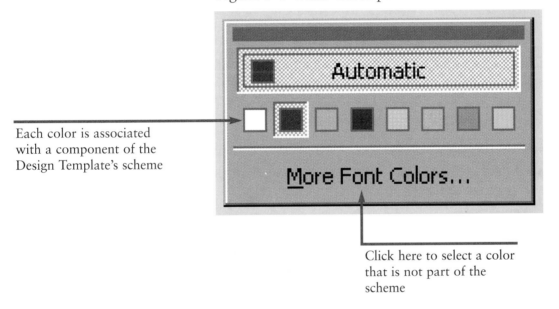

Each color is associated with a component of the Design Template's scheme

Click here to select a color that is not part of the scheme

Figure 3-7 Formatted title text

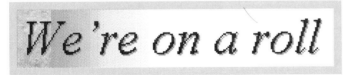

# Formatting Text (continued)

## Do It!

**12** Scroll toward the beginning of the list and click the font named Arial. The typeface of the new accounts will change from Times New Roman to Arial.

**13** Click the text label **Recently Acquired Accounts** to activate the text box, then triple-click the text to select the entire line.

**14** Click the Increase Font Size button **A** twice. The point size will increase to 32.

**15** Click the Font box (not the arrow). The current font will be highlighted.

**16** Type Arial, then press [Enter]. The text will change fonts. If the text label runs off the slide, click the text box's border and drag it to the left so the entire text box is within the boundaries of the slide. The Font and Font Size boxes are text boxes. If you know exactly what typeface or size you want your text to be you can enter this information from the keyboard; you are not limited to using the drop-down list.

**17** Click the Font Color button (not the arrow). Clicking the button itself applies the last color you chose from the Font Color palette to the selected text. This color is displayed as part of the button's icon so that you know which color is loaded.

**18** Click the Underline button **U**. A line will appear under the text. Whenever this text is selected, the Underline button will be indented, indicating that it is active.

**19** Deselect the active text box. Your formatted slide should look like **Figure 3-8**.

**20** Save your presentation.

## More

If the exact point size that you want to apply to selected text is not available on the Font Size drop-down list, you can type any whole number between 1 and 4000 into the Font Size text box. The point size of the selected text will be changed to reflect your entry.

If you need to apply several formatting changes to a selection of text, you may want to use the Font dialog box, which can be opened by choosing the Font command from the Format menu. The Font dialog box, shown in **Figure 3-9**, allows you to view all of the characteristics of the selected text at once. It also offers additional formatting options that are not available on the Formatting toolbar. These include the ability to apply an Emboss effect and to set text as subscript or super-script.

Figure 3-8 Slide with formatted text

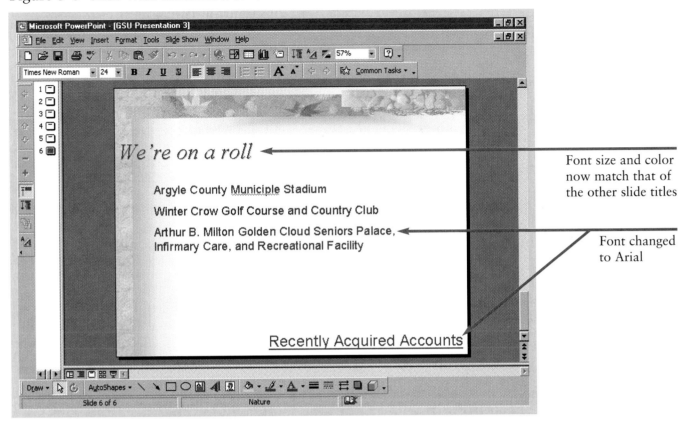

Font size and color now match that of the other slide titles

Font changed to Arial

Figure 3-9 Font dialog box

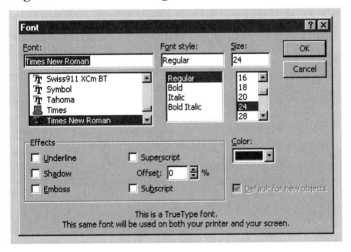

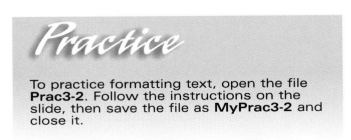

**Practice**

To practice formatting text, open the file **Prac3-2**. Follow the instructions on the slide, then save the file as **MyPrac3-2** and close it.

**Hot Tip**

You can select an entire sentence by pressing **[Ctrl]** and clicking any portion of it.

 # Moving Text Boxes and Aligning Text

### Concept

To improve the appearance of a slide's layout, text boxes can be moved and the text inside them can be realigned. You can move text boxes easily by dragging them or by pressing the arrow keys. The four basic text alignment options are left, center, right, and justify. In addition to aligning text according to the boundaries of its text box, you can adjust the spacing between paragraphs in a text box.

### Do It!

Trista wants to move the text boxes on her sixth slide and align the main text.

**1** Click the title text, We're On A Roll, to activate the text box. Small boxes called sizing handles will appear at the corners and at the center of each side of the frame.

**2** Position the pointer over the hashed border. It will change to ⬨. Then, click on the frame (not on a handle) and drag to the right until the dashed box representing the text box is centered just below the decorative band at the top of the slide. When you release the mouse button, the actual text box will relocate.

**3** Click the main body text, the account names, to select its text box.

**4** Click the hashed border to activate the frame instead of the text. Then press the down arrow key repeatedly to move the text box into the lower half of the slide.

**5** Select the Recently Acquired Accounts text box, and use the mouse to drag it to its proper place, between the title and account names, as shown in **Figure 3-10**.

**6** Click the text box containing the names of the new accounts. Select all of the text by clicking before the first letter of the first line and then holding [Shift] while clicking after the last letter of the last line.

**7** Click the Center button 🔳 on the Formatting toolbar. The selected text will align itself evenly between the borders of the text box.

**8** Click the More Buttons ⬤ arrow at the end of the Formatting toolbar, then point to the Add or Remove Buttons command. A menu of buttons will appear. Click Increase Paragraph Spacing to add its button to the toolbar.

**9** Click the Increase Paragraph Spacing button 🔳 four times. The space between each account name will increase. Click anywhere to deselect the text. Your slide should appear similar to the one shown in **Figure 3-11**.

**10** Save and close your presentation.

### More

You can resize an active text box by dragging one of its sizing handles. When you place the mouse pointer over a sizing handle, it will change to a double-arrow that shows the directions in which that handle can be moved. Handles at the corners of a frame can be used to adjust the size of the box in two directions, while the handles on the sides only influence either the height or width.

Figure 3-10 Repositioned text boxes

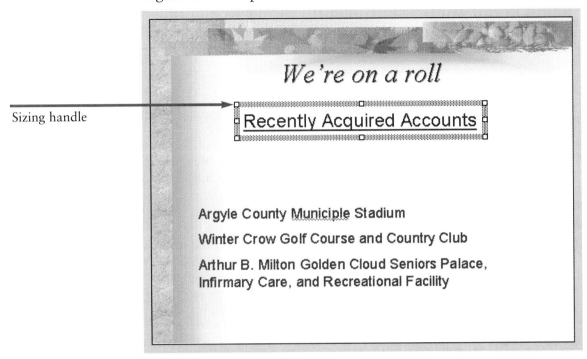

Sizing handle

Figure 3-11 Center aligned text

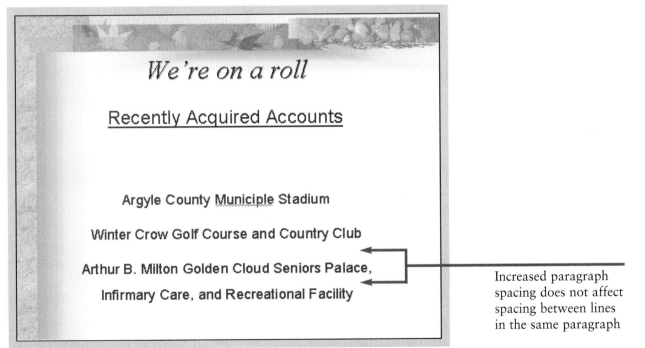

Increased paragraph spacing does not affect spacing between lines in the same paragraph

## Practice

Open **Prac3-3** and follow the instructions on the slide. Save the file as **MyPrac3-3** when you are done.

## Hot Tip

You can resize a text box while maintaining its proportions by holding **[Shift]** while you drag a corner sizing handle.

# Using Spell Check

## Concept

Even the most careful workers can make typing mistakes that they will not catch with their own eyes. PowerPoint has a Spell Check feature that finds spelling errors in a presentation and offers you choices for fixing them. Be aware that Spell Check cannot determine if a word has been misused, such as "there" instead of "their." Also, it will tag any words that it does not recognize, including some proper names and most words in other languages.

## Do It!

Trista wants to check for misspelled words in her presentation.

1. With the presentation still on Slide 6, click the Spelling button [ABC] on the Standard toolbar. The Spelling dialog box, shown in **Figure 3-12**, appears. The first questionable word it has found, Municiple, is displayed in the Not in Dictionary: box. The Change to: box contains the first of the two suggested replacements for the misspelled word, which are shown in the Suggestions: box.

2. Click the Change button [ Change ] to change Municiple to the suggested, and correct spelling, Municipal. The correction is made, and the Spelling dialog box advances to the next questionable word it finds in the presentation, which is on Slide 3. The word is also highlighted on the slide itself (see **Figure 3-13**).

3. The next suspect word that appears in the Not in Dictionary: box is part of the scientific name of one of the grass varieties grown by Green Side Up. It has been flagged because PowerPoint's dictionary does not recognize the word. However, it is spelled correctly. Click the Ignore button [ Ignore ] to leave the word unchanged and advance to the next questionable word.

4. Click [ Ignore ] seven more times to ignore the remaining names that PowerPoint does not recognize. When you have finished, a dialog box will appear to inform you that the check is complete. Notice that all the red wavy lines have disappeared.

5. Click [ OK ] to exit the Spell Check and return to your presentation. Save the file to preserve the spelling changes.

## More

Clicking [ Ignore ] tells PowerPoint to leave an unrecognized word unchanged and move to the next misspelled word. It will stop if it finds that same word again in the file. If you click [ Ignore All ], however, PowerPoint will skip any additional instances of that particular word. Likewise, the [ Change All ] button will change every instance of the word in question to whatever is in the Change To: text box. Ordinarily, PowerPoint places its primary suggested change directly into the Change To: box; you may click another of its suggestions or type a new word to replace the original suggestion. In the example above, PowerPoint recognized several names but failed to recognize the names of the grass varieties. If these were names that you were going to use often, you could add them to PowerPoint's custom dictionary so that they would no longer be questioned by the Spell Checker. Just click the Add button [ Add ] to "teach" PowerPoint the word in question. The custom dictionary is a document unique to each copy of PowerPoint that consists solely of words that have been added to it during the Spell Check process.

Figure 3-12  Spelling dialog box

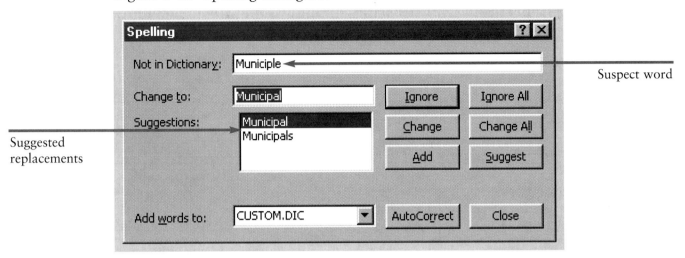

Suspect word

Suggested replacements

Figure 3-13  Suspect word highlighted

Suspected misspelling is highlighted so you can see it in its proper context

*Practice*

Open practice file **Prac3-4** and use PowerPoint's Spelling dialog box to find and correct the errors it contains. When you have finished, close the file and save it to your student disk as **MyPrac3-4**.

*Hot Tip*

You can change the language used by the Spell Check by selecting the Language command from the Tools menu.

# Replacing Text

## Concept

If there is a specific change you would like to make to a word or phrase throughout your presentation, PowerPoint offers a Find and Replace function that saves you from conducting long manual searches. You can view each instance of the desired item and change them individually, or instruct PowerPoint to change all instances of the item at once.

## Do It!

Trista wants to find and replace a statistical error she has made in her presentation.

1. Click Edit, then click Replace (you may have to wait a moment for the Replace command to appear). The Replace dialog box opens with a blinking insertion point in the Find what: box.

2. Type the number 1217, and then press [Tab] to move the insertion point into the Replace with: box.

3. Type the number 1322, as shown in **Figure 3-14**.

4. Click the Find Next button [Find Next]. PowerPoint highlights the first occurrence (beginning from the active slide) of the entry in the Find what: box on the slide on which it appears, as shown in **Figure 3-15**.

5. Click the Replace All button [Replace All] to replace all occurrences of the number 1217 with 1322. A dialog box appears with the results of the Find and Replace operation (see **Figure 3-16**).

6. Click [OK] to continue.

7. Close the Replace dialog box and save your changes.

## More

When you are working with a presentation that contains multiple slides, the Replace command can be used to search the entire presentation at once. To replace a word on a case by case basis, click the Replace button [Replace] in the Replace dialog box instead of the Replace All button. The Find dialog box is similar to the Replace dialog box except that it lacks the Replace function and merely searches your presentation for items you specify. This is useful if you wish to find out how many times you used certain words in your presentation, or if you need to go to a specific word or item in a presentation, but do not know the slide on which it is located. Clicking [Replace...] transforms the Find dialog box into the Replace dialog box.

Figure 3-14 Replace dialog box

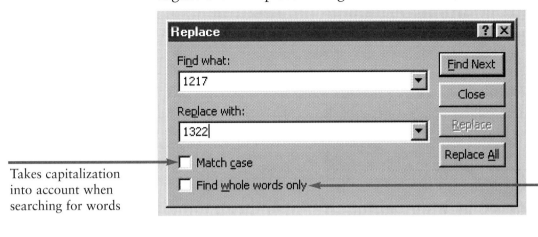

Takes capitalization
into account when
searching for words

Instructs PowerPoint
to ignore requested
word when it is part
of another word

Figure 3-15 Found word highlighted

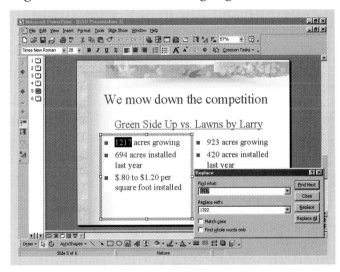

Figure 3-16 Find and Replace confirmation

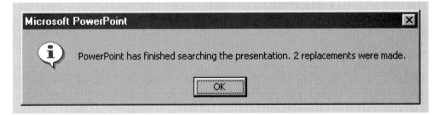

*Practice*

Open **Prac3-5** and follow the instructions on the slide. Save the file as **MyPrac3-5** when you are done.

*Hot Tip*

The Find what: and Replace with: text boxes have drop-down lists that contain your previous Find and Replace entries so that you can conduct repeat searches quickly.

# Using AutoCorrect

## Concept

PowerPoint's **AutoCorrect** feature takes the idea of a Spell Check one step further. In addition to finding your spelling errors, AutoCorrect fixes them as soon as you type them. The feature recognizes a predetermined set of common typing errors such as "teh" for "the." However, you can customize AutoCorrect to act upon specific words that you frequently enter incorrectly.

## Do It!

Trista wants to set AutoCorrect to automatically fix a typing mistake that she frequently makes.

**1** Click the New button ⬜ to create a new file. The New Slide dialog box opens.

**2** Select a Title Only slide and click ⬜ OK ⬜. The new slide appears in the document window.

**3** Click Tools, then click AutoCorrect. The AutoCorrect dialog box opens with the insertion point in the Replace: box, as shown in **Figure 3-17**.

**4** Type the word presentatoin. The word is misspelled here intentionally.

**5** Press [Tab] to move the insertion point to the With: box.

**6** Type presentation. PowerPoint will now replace the word "presentatoin" with "presentation" whenever it is entered on a PowerPoint slide.

**7** Click ⬜ OK ⬜ to accept the changes you have made and to leave the AutoCorrect dialog box. The slide that you created earlier is now in the active window.

**8** Click the Title text box to activate it, and type presentatoin, followed by a space. Notice that when the space bar is pressed, indicating that you have finished the word, PowerPoint automatically fixes the mistake. It also capitalizes the word, as it recognizes it to be the first word of a sentence (see **Figure 3-18**).

**9** Close the file. You do not need to save it.

## More

Any word following a paragraph mark ¶ or a period and a space is capitalized automatically, as PowerPoint recognizes it to be the first word of a sentence. To keep PowerPoint from capitalizing words after abbreviations, the AutoCorrect dialog box has a list of Exceptions, accessible by clicking ⬜ Exceptions... ⬜ in the AutoCorrect dialog box, that it will take into account when determining if a new sentence has been started. Entries may be added to or removed from the Exceptions list as needed. Other AutoCorrect options include automatic capitalization of days of the week, and correcting the accidental use of two capital letters at the beginning of a word. To get rid of an AutoCorrect entry that you do not want, select the entry where it appears in the AutoCorrect dialog box and click ⬜ Delete ⬜.

Figure 3-17  AutoCorrect dialog box

Additional AutoCorrect options

Turns AutoCorrect on and off

AutoCorrect will convert certain character combinations into commonly used symbols

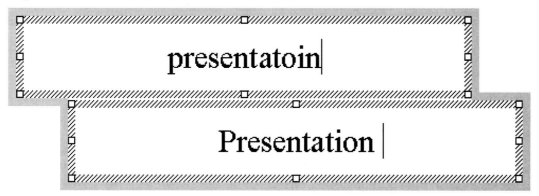

Figure 3-18  Text correct with AutoCorrect

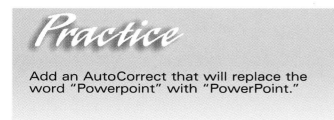

**Practice**

Add an AutoCorrect that will replace the word "Powerpoint" with "PowerPoint."

**Hot Tip**

If you turn off AutoCorrect, you can still use PowerPoint's Spell Check feature to catch the common mistakes that AutoCorrect would have corrected.

 # Drawing and Formatting Objects

## Concept

Including drawings in your presentation helps capture the viewer's interest and imagination. PowerPoint's Drawing toolbar has tools for lines, shapes, pictures, and other graphical objects. You have complete control over where these items are placed and how much space they will occupy on a slide. Once you draw an object, you can modify virtually all aspects of it using editing and formatting techniques.

## Do It!

Trista wants to create an arrow with a color gradient to enhance her presentation's Title Slide.

1. Open GSU Presentation 3 to **Slide 1**.

2. Click the **AutoShapes** button `AutoShapes ▾` on the Drawing toolbar. The AutoShapes menu will appear.

3. Highlight **Block Arrows**, then click the **Up Arrow** button ⬆ on the submenu that appears (see **Figure 3-19**). The mouse pointer will change to a crosshairs pointer when you move it over the presentation window.

4. With the crosshairs, click the upper-right corner of the slide and drag down and to the left, creating an arrow that has the approximate dimensions of the one in **Figure 3-20**. When you let go of the mouse button the arrow will appear filled, with seven sizing handles (white squares), and one adjustment handle (yellow diamond).

5. Click the **Fill Color** drop-down arrow ⬙▾ on the Drawing toolbar. The Fill Color palette will appear with color choices and commands that allow you to view more Fill Colors or Fill Effects.

6. Click **Fill Effects**. The Fill Effects dialog box will appear.

7. Click the **Gradient** tab to bring it to the front of the dialog box if it is not already there.

Figure 3-19  Choosing an AutoShape

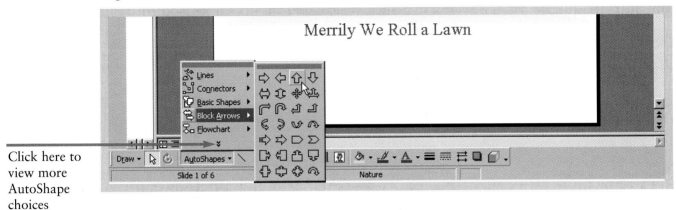

Click here to
view more
AutoShape
choices

Figure 3-20  Drawing an AutoShape

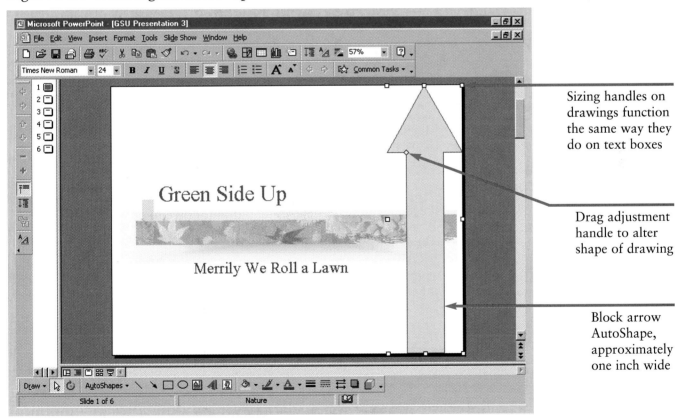

Sizing handles on
drawings function
the same way they
do on text boxes

Drag adjustment
handle to alter
shape of drawing

Block arrow
AutoShape,
approximately
one inch wide

PowerPoint 2000

# Drawing and Formatting Objects
## (continued)

**Do It!**

8  Click the Two colors radio button. Drop-down list boxes labeled Color 1: and Color 2: appear, as shown in **Figure 3-21**. These are used to select the two colors that will make up the Fill Color gradient.

9  Click the Color 2: drop-down list arrow, then select the green color box, second from the right on the color palette (its ScreenTip will say **Follow Accent and Hyperlink Scheme Color** when you point to it). Notice that the Sample: box changes to incorporate the new color into the gradient.

10  Leave the Shading styles and Variants sections set to their default options.

11  Click the Preview button [Preview] to see how the gradient looks when applied to the AutoShape.

12  Click [OK] to add the gradient and close the Fill Effects dialog box.

13  Click anywhere outside the slide to deselect the arrow. The slide should now resemble **Figure 3-22**.

14  Save the changes to your file.

**More**

The Texture tab in the Fill Effects dialog box provides a palette of textures, such as marble or wood, that can be applied to objects you create. The Pattern tab is similar to the Texture tab, but instead provides 42 simple patterns from which you can choose. The Picture tab allows you to fill an object with a picture or other graphic that you have on file.

You can rotate objects that you have created using the Free Rotate tool available on the Drawing toolbar. Simply select the object you wish to rotate, then click the Free Rotate button [↻]. Green circles will appear at the corners of the selected object that you can drag to rotate it. Ordinarily, an object will rotate about its center. When [Ctrl] is pressed while rotating, however, the object will rotate about the corner opposite the one being dragged. Objects can be freely rotated to any degree you wish, or the rotation can be constrained to 15° increments by holding [Shift] while you drag.

You can rotate an object in 90° increments or flip it horizontally or vertically by using the commands on the Rotate or Flip submenu of the Draw menu, which is located at the left end of the Drawing toolbar.

Figure 3-21  Fill Effects dialog box

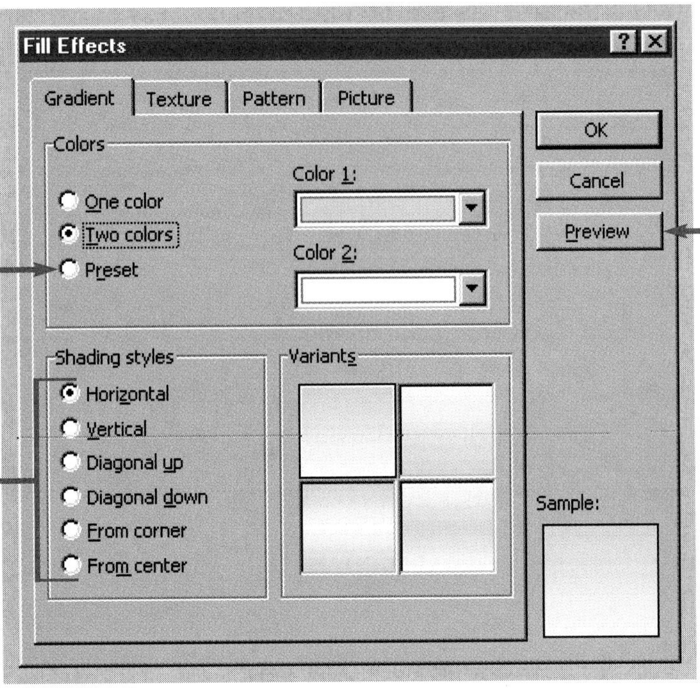

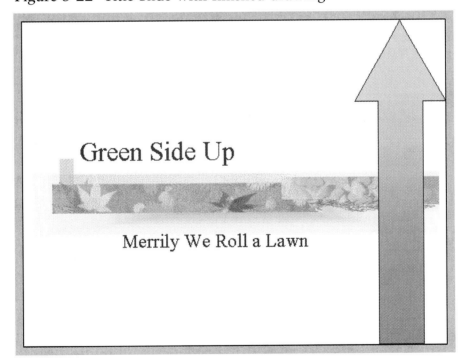

Allows you to choose pre-made gradients with descriptive names like Late Sunset and Ocean

Shading styles determine orientation of the gradient

Click to apply the selected gradient temporarily without closing the dialog box

Figure 3-22  Title Slide with finished drawing

*Practice*

Open **Prac3-7** and follow the instructions on the slide. Save the file as **MyPrac3-7** when you are done.

*Hot Tip*

You can double-click a drawn object to open a Format dialog box tailored specifically for that object.

# Modifying and Enhancing Drawn Objects

## Concept

Occasionally when you add a drawn object to a presentation, it does not accomplish exactly what you had imagined it would. Fortunately, drawings such as AutoShapes can be modified so that they work better within the scheme of a slide. This includes enhancing the object itself and changing how the object interacts with the other elements on the slide.

## Do It!

Trista wants to add a shadow to the AutoShape she drew on her Title Slide.

1. Click the Block Arrow on Slide 1 to select it.

2. Click the Shadow button 🔲 on the Drawing toolbar. A menu of shadow types will appear.

3. Click Shadow Style 3, the third shadow in the first row. A shadow will be cast from the Block Arrow's base through the middle of the slide, as shown in **Figure 3-23**.

4. Click the Draw button Draw ▾ on the Drawing toolbar to open the Draw menu.

5. Highlight the Order command on the Draw menu to open its submenu. The Order submenu contains commands that allow you to layer the objects on your slides according to your needs. Since the Block Arrow was the last object you added, it is on the top layer in the order, and its shadow is blocking the subtitle text Merrily We Roll a Lawn.

6. Click Send to Back on the Order submenu. The Arrow and its shadow are sent to the back of the order, revealing the text that was hidden (see **Figure 3-24**). Notice that the shadow still passes in front of the decorative band in the middle of the slide. The order of elements that are part of the Design Template cannot be changed, so they will always be behind any elements you add.

7. Deselect the Block Arrow and save your file.

## More

Even though a shadow is part of the object to which it has been applied, some aspects of a shadow can be modified independently. With the object selected, click the Shadow button 🔲, and then click the Shadow Settings command. The Shadow Settings toolbar, shown in **Figure 3-25**, will appear. The buttons on this toolbar allow you to turn a shadow on or off, nudge it up, down, left, or right, and change its color and opacity.

The Send Backward command enables you to send an object down one place in the layering order rather than all the way to the bottom layer. The Send to Front and Send Forward commands mirror the Send to Back and Send Backward commands.

Figure 3-23  Adding a shadow to a drawing

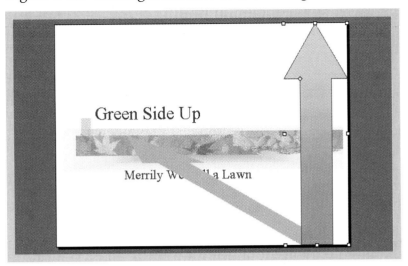

Figure 3-24  Arrow and shadow sent to back

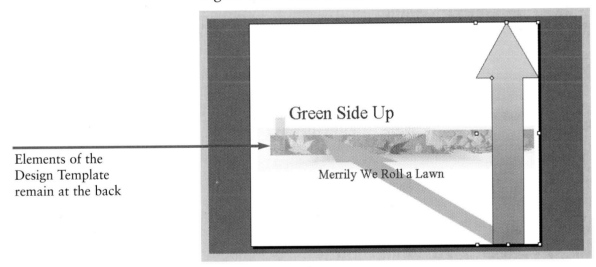

Elements of the
Design Template
remain at the back

Figure 3-25  Shadow Settings toolbar

Depressed button
indicates shadow is on

Click to change shadow color

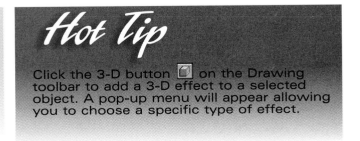

*Practice*

Open **Prac3-8** and follow the instructions on the slide. Save the file as **MyPrac3-8** when you are done.

*Hot Tip*

Click the 3-D button 🗖 on the Drawing toolbar to add a 3-D effect to a selected object. A pop-up menu will appear allowing you to choose a specific type of effect.

# Shortcuts

| Function | Button/Mouse | Menu | Keyboard |
|---|---|---|---|
| Bold text | B | Click Format, then Font, and select Bold | [Ctrl]+[B] |
| Italicize text | I | Click Format, then Font, and select Italic | [Ctrl]+[I] |
| Underline text | U | Click Format, then Font, and select Underline | [Ctrl]+[U] |
| Apply Text Shadow | S | Click Format, then Font, and select Shadow | |
| Center alignment | ≡ | Click Format, then highlight Alignment, then click Center | [Ctrl]+[E] |
| Align Left | ≣ | Click Format, then highlight Alignment, then click Align Left | [Ctrl]+[L] |
| Right alignment | ≣ | Click Format, then highlight Alignment, then click Align Right | [Ctrl]+[R] |
| Spelling | ABC✓ | Click Tools, then click Spelling | [F7] |
| Increase font size | A | Click Format, then click Font | [Ctrl]+[Shift]+[>] |
| Decrease font size | A | Click Format, then click Font | [Ctrl]+[Shift]+[<] |

## Identify Key Features

Name the items indicated by callout arrows in **Figure 3-26**.

Figure 3-26 Elements of the Formatting and Drawing toolbars

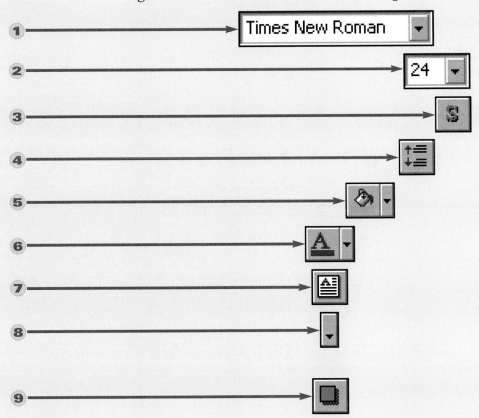

## Select The Best Answer

10. Fixes spelling errors automatically as you type

11. Allows you to ignore or change a misspelled word

12. Leads to a list of abbreviations after which the next word will not be capitalized

13. Offers a full range of text formatting options

14. Allows you to teach PowerPoint words it does not know so that they will not be marked as misspelled

15. Contains options for filling an object with a gradient

16. An example of an AutoShape

17. Permits you to make global changes to a presentation's text

a. Block Arrow

b. Font dialog box

c. Replace All button

d. AutoCorrect

e. Fill Effects dialog box

f. Spelling dialog box

g. Add button

h. Exceptions button

## Complete the Statement

18. A text box that automatically wraps to the next line when the insertion point reaches its boundary is a:

    a. Text label text box

    b. Title text box

    c. Flex box

    d. Word processing text box

19. To move an object to the top level of a slide, choose the:

    a. Send Forward command

    b. Send Backward command

    c. Send to Front command

    d. Send to Back command

20. The Replace command is found:

    a. In the Spelling dialog box

    b. On the Edit menu

    c. On the Standard toolbar

    d. On the Editing toolbar

21. The text alignment option that is not available on the Standard toolbar is:

    a. Left

    b. Right

    c. Center

    d. Justify

22. If you are adding a single word or short phrase to a slide, it is best to use a:

    a. Text label text box

    b. Word processing text box

    c. Text shadow

    d. Bold font

23. The Rotate or Flip and Order commands are located on the:

    a. Standard toolbar

    b. Edit menu

    c. Formatting toolbar

    d. Draw menu

24. All of the following control font size except the:

    a. Font box

    b. Font Size box

    c. Increase/Decrease Font Size buttons

    d. Font dialog box

25. The yellow diamond attached to a selected object is called the:

    a. Sizing handle

    b. Adjustment handle

    c. Move handle

    d. Free Rotate tool

# Interactivity

## Test Your Skills

1. Practice entering and moving text:

   a. Open a new File starting with a Blank presentation.

   b. Choose a blank slide for your first slide.

   c. Apply the design Notebook to the presentation.

   d. Use the Text Box button to create a text label box in the middle of the slide.

   e. In the box type My Family.

   f. Move the text box above the solid line near the top of the slide, and to the left side.

   g. Click the Text Box button again, and drag a large word processing box in the area of the slide below the line.

   h. Type a brief history of your family in this text box.

2. Practice formatting text:

   a. Click the My Family text box to activate it.

   b. Drag the sizing handle in the middle of the right side to the right edge of the slide's light area.

   c. Center the text.

   d. Make the text bold, and increase its size to 40 point.

   e. Click the lower text box to activate it.

   f. Increase the paragraph spacing slightly, and italicize the text.

3. Build and refine your presentation:

   a. Using the Blank Slide AutoLayout, add a slide for each member of your family.

   b. Format each slide as you did the first one, replacing My Family with the family member's name, and the brief history with a description of the family member.

   c. Format the text on each of the new slides with a different color.

   d. Use Find and Replace to replace all instances of the phrase My Family with The [Insert Last Name] Family.

   e. When you are done, Spell Check the presentation. If your last name is not in PowerPoint's dictionary, add it to the Custom dictionary.

PowerPoint 2000

# Interactivity (continued)

4. Add, format, and modify drawing objects:

   a. Select the AutoShape 5-Point Star.

   b. Draw the 5-Point Star on Slide 1 of your presentation, adjusting the size and location of the slide's text boxes if necessary.

   c. Fill the star with a Two color gradient that uses the Vertical Shading style and consists of the Fills Scheme Color and the Accent Scheme Color.

   d. Apply Shadow Style 2 to the star.

   e. Draw the 32-Point Star AutoShape over the 5-Point Star, slightly larger.

   f. Change the color of the 32-Point Star to the Accent Scheme Color.

   g. Use the Order command to move the 32-Point Star behind the 5-Point Star.

---

## Problem Solving

1. After years of toiling at an unfulfilling nine to five job, you have finally saved enough money to quit and realize your dream of opening a small country inn. Use PowerPoint to create an eight slide introductory brochure that you can show to some of the investors who are helping you get your new business started. Since the inn is still in its planning stages, the presentation will consist mostly of text that describes what the inn will look like, where it will be located, the general atmosphere you hope to provide, and other kinds of information that would be important to travelers. Use text formatting, AutoShapes, and Fill Colors to make the brochure interesting and lively. Be sure to check your presentation for spelling errors. Save the presentation as Solved3-1.ppt.

2. Peppercorn's, a national chain of steakhouses, has hired you to do some freelance design work for their advertising department. The company is launching a print advertising campaign that will place adds in five major magazines. They want to use a different half-page ad in each of the five magazines so that the ads are geared toward specific readers. You have been asked to provide first drafts of the five ads in the form of a PowerPoint presentation so the Director of Advertising can preview them. The five magazines that will be running the ads are Sports Digest, Women's Quarterly, Men Today, Entertainment Extract, and News Now. Save your presentation as Solved3-2.ppt.

*Interactivity (continued)*

3. Use PowerPoint to recreate the slide shown in **Figure PS3a**. Then make the appropriate changes to the slide so that it resembles **Figure PS3b**. Print a copy of each slide.

Figure PS3a

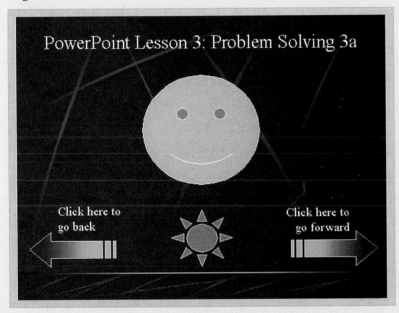

Figure PS3b

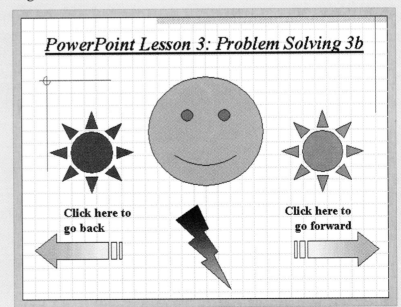

# Interactivity (continued)

4. Use PowerPoint to recreate the slide shown in **Figure PS4a**. Then make the appropriate changes to the slide so that it resembles **Figure PS4b**. Print a copy of each slide.

Figure PS4a

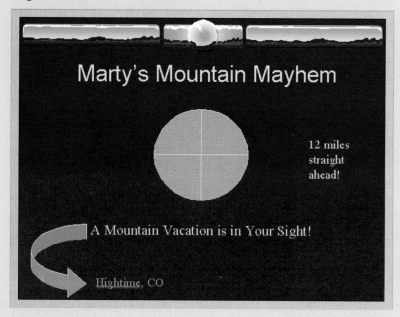

Figure PS4b

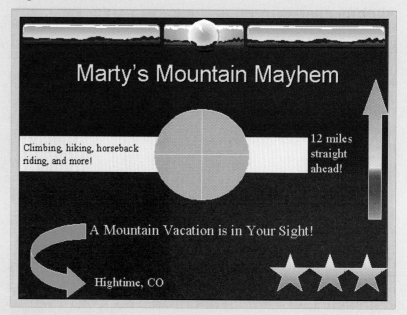

L E S S O N

# 4

# STRENGTHENING YOUR PRESENTATION

Astrong presentation requires more than just text and simple shapes to make it an interesting and visually stimulating slide show. You can enhance your presentation with detailed pictures provided by PowerPoint called Clip Art. Once you insert a piece of Clip Art, you will find that you can edit and format it so that it is compatible with your particular presentation. You will also learn how to insert your own image files into a presentation.

Another important visual aspect of a presentation is the manner in which data is represented. Raw statistics serve an important purpose, but sometimes lack effectiveness when presented as such. PowerPoint allows you to create graphical charts to display any kind of data. Different chart types, such as line, bar, or pie, are available so you can choose the type that fits your data best. Once you have created a chart, you can control its placement on the slide, the colors and sizes of individual chart objects, its text style, and its overall size.

The end product of most PowerPoint presentations is a slide show, where the slides are displayed with all of the graphics, text, and other features that were included in their creation. Though a presentation can be created solely for the purpose of producing paper copies or overhead transparencies, PowerPoint's true strengths show through when the slides are animated and presented on a computer screen. Using the program's slide transition features, you can control exactly how each slide will make its appearance on the screen, and how much time it will remain there before the presentation advances to the next slide. You can also predetermine whether slides will advance on their own or with a prompt from the presenter.

### CASE STUDY
In this lesson, Trista will add pictures to her presentation, both from Microsoft's Clip Gallery and from her own file. She will also transform raw data she has accumulated into a chart, and then customize the chart to her needs and preferences. Finally, she will add transition effects to her slides and set slide timings.

# Adding Clip Art

**Concept**

You have already seen how you can enhance your presentation by drawing objects such as AutoShapes. To take the visual aspect of your presentation a step further, you may want to use Clip Art. Clip Art is a collection of ready-made pictures that PowerPoint provides for the user. Clip Art pictures are more numerous, varied, and generally more detailed than drawings created with AutoShapes.

**Do It!**

Trista would like to add Clip Art to her presentation.

**1** Open **GSU Presentation 3** and save it as **GSU Presentation 4**.

**2** Go to **Slide 2** in the presentation, the slide titled Growing to meet your needs.

**3** Click **Insert**, then highlight **Picture**, then click **Clip Art**. The Insert Clip Art dialog box will open. If the dialog box that appears on your screen is tall and thin and only displays one column of categories, click the **Change to Full Window** ⬛ button so that the dialog box looks like **Figure 4-1**. The Pictures tab contains 57 categories of pictures that you can browse by clicking their icons. You can also search for a specific type of picture.

**4** Click the text in the **Search for clips:** text box to select it. Then type **ribbons** and press **[Enter]**. PowerPoint will search the Clip Gallery for a picture that matches the description, and display its findings on the tab.

**5** Place the mouse pointer over the picture of a man holding a red prize ribbon. A ScreenTip containing the picture's name and file size will appear.

**6** Click the red ribbon picture. A menu will appear beside it, giving you several options (see **Figure 4-2**).

**7** Click the top button on the menu, **Insert clip** ⬛. Then close the dialog box. The picture will appear on the slide, as shown in **Figure 4-3**.

**More**

If you know that a particular slide in your presentation will include Clip Art, you can choose an AutoLayout slide that is designed for that purpose. For example, if you add a **Text and Clip Art** slide to your presentation, it will include a placeholder for inserting Clip Art as part of its AutoLayout. When you double-click on the placeholder, the **Microsoft Clip Gallery** will open.

The Insert Clip Art dialog box is completely customizable. To move a clip from one category to another, select the clip, click the **Copy** button ⬛, select the new category, and then click the **Paste** button ⬛. You can also move or copy a picture file from another storage location into the Insert Clip Art dialog box by clicking the **Import Clips** button ⬛ Import Clips . Finally, if you have an Internet connection, you can access additional clips by clicking the **Clips Online** button ⬛ Clips Online . This will connect you to the **Microsoft Clip Gallery Live**, which allows you to download clips from Microsoft's Web site to the Insert Clip Art dialog box.

Figure 4-1  Insert Clip Art dialog box

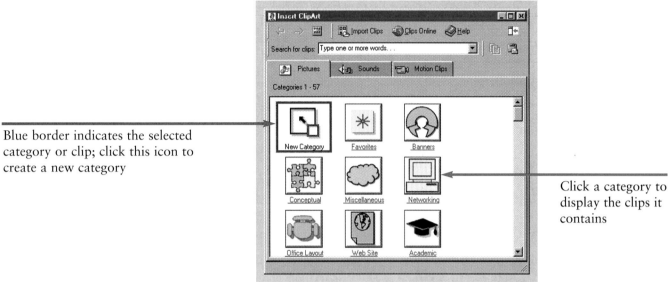

Blue border indicates the selected category or clip; click this icon to create a new category

Click a category to display the clips it contains

Figure 4-2  Inserting Clip Art

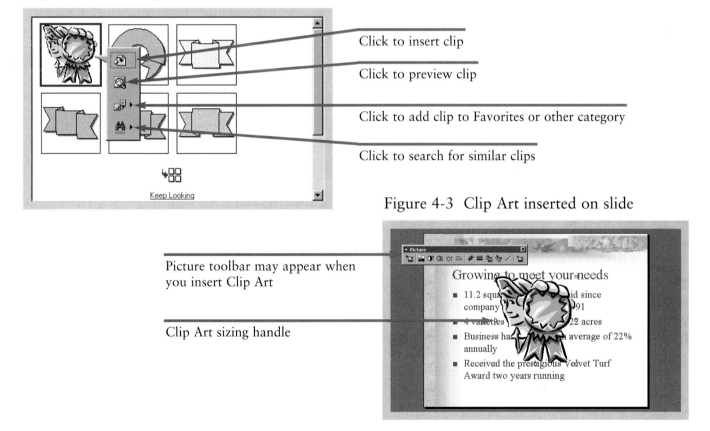

Click to insert clip

Click to preview clip

Click to add clip to Favorites or other category

Click to search for similar clips

Figure 4-3  Clip Art inserted on slide

Picture toolbar may appear when you insert Clip Art

Clip Art sizing handle

Open the file **Prac4-1** and follow the instructions on the slide. Save the file as **MyPrac4-1**.

## Hot Tip

The standard installation of PowerPoint does not provide files for the **Sounds** and **Motion Clips** tabs in the Insert Clip Art dialog box. You can add your own files or download clips from the Microsoft Clip Gallery Live.

# Editing Clip Art

**Concept**

Clip Art files are quality, finished pictures. They have particular dimensions and colors that are part of the file. However, like other objects you insert into a PowerPoint slide, they can be repositioned, resized, and reformatted to fit the slide on which they appear. Most characteristics of a piece of Clip Art can be altered by using the Picture toolbar.

**Do It!**

Trista wants to resize the ribbon Clip Art she inserted and move it to its appropriate place on the slide. Then she will change the picture's color so it matches the scheme of her presentation.

1.  The Clip Art you inserted in the last Skill should still be selected on Slide 2 (simply click the picture if it is not selected). If the Picture toolbar is not active, click View, then highlight Toolbars, and click Picture on the submenu.

2.  Click the Format Picture ⌗ button on the Picture toolbar. The Format Picture dialog box will open.

3.  Click the Size tab to bring it to the front of the dialog box. The Size and rotate section of the tab allows you to adjust the height and width of the picture using linear measurements such as inches. The Scale section of the tab allows you to adjust the height and width as a percentage of the picture's original size, which is displayed at the bottom of the tab. When the Lock aspect ratio check box is checked, changing the height will alter the width in the proper proportion, and vice-versa (activate this check box now if necessary).

4.  Double-click the current value in the Scale section's Height: box, 100%, to select it.

5.  Type the number 50 to replace the original value, as shown in **Figure 4-4**.

6.  Click ⌗OK⌗ to close the dialog box and make the Scale change. Though you didn't see it change, the value in the Width: box was also changed from 100% to 50% because the aspect ration was locked. The Clip Art picture should now appear on the slide at half its original size (see **Figure 4-5**).

7.  Place the mouse pointer over the picture and hold down the mouse button. Then drag down and to the right until the outline of the picture is directly below the phrase Velvet Turf. Release the mouse button to drop the picture in its proper place, as shown in **Figure 4-6**. Notice that the picture runs over the bottom edge of the slide.

8.  Click ⌗ again to return to the Format Picture dialog box. In the Size tab's Size and rotate section, click the down arrow in the Height: box until the value reaches 1.49". Notice that the Width: box value and the percentages in the Scale section change as well.

9.  Click ⌗OK⌗. The picture now fits neatly on the slide.

Figure 4-4 Format Picture dialog box

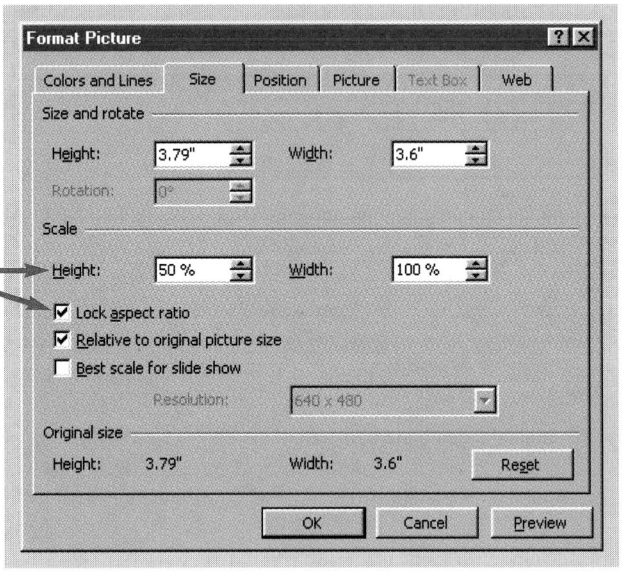

Adjusting height changes width in the proper proportion because aspect ratio is locked

Figure 4-5  Scaled Clip Art

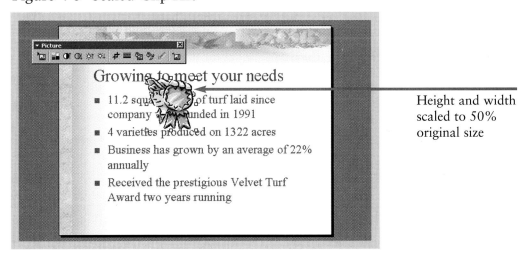

Height and width scaled to 50% original size

Figure 4-6  Moving Clip Art

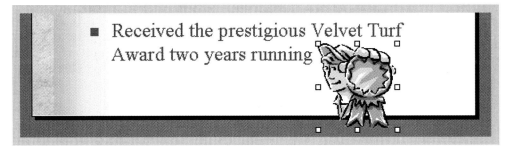

# Editing Clip Art
# (continued)

**Do It!**

**10** Click the Recolor Picture button 📷 on the Picture toolbar. The Recolor Picture dialog box will appear. The dialog box, shown in **Figure 4-7**, consists of a series of boxes that display every color used in the picture. Next to each of these boxes is a corresponding selection box that allows you to change a color everywhere that it appears in the picture. The right half of the dialog box lets you preview how your color changes will look before you actually apply them to the picture.

**11** Click the Fills radio button in the Change section of the dialog box. This excludes lines from the list of items you can change, leaving only background and fill colors available for editing.

**12** Click the arrow on the right end of the third color box listed in the New: column (this is the color of the ribbon itself). A color palette will appear.

**13** Click Automatic to select your Design Template's Automatic Fill Color (light blue).

**14** Change the fourth orignal color listed (red) to the fourth color on the palette (dark blue, Follow Title Text Scheme Color).

**15** Click ▭ OK ▭ to make the color changes and close the dialog box.

**16** Close the Picture toolbar and deselect the picture. Your slide should resemble **Figure 4-8**.

**17** Save the changes you have made to your presentation.

**More**

In the preceding exercise, you used the Format Picture dialog box's Size tab to resize a Clip Art picture. If you are not concerned about exact measurements, you can resize Clip Art by dragging its sizing handles, just like other objects. The Crop tool 🔲 available on the Picture toolbar lets you hide part of a graphic from view. Using this tool you can adjust a picture's frame without resizing the image at the same time, and thereby use the frame to cut off portions of the graphic you do not wish to display.

Figure 4-7  Recolor Picture dialog box

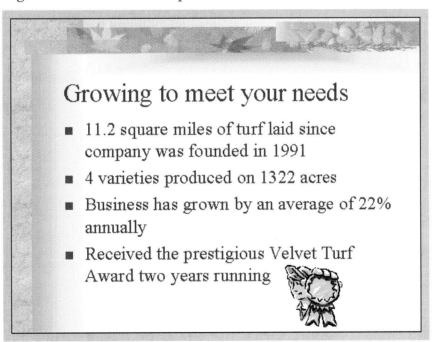

Allows you to change all colors including lines

Color changes are reflected in Preview box

Figure 4-8  Recolored Clip Art

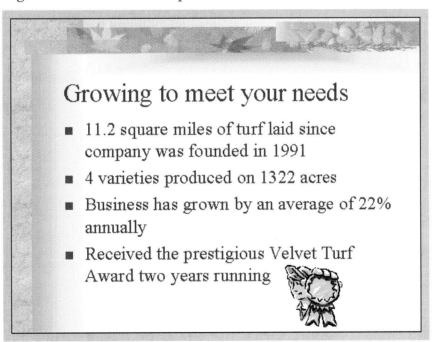

# Growing to meet your needs

- 11.2 square miles of turf laid since company was founded in 1991
- 4 varieties produced on 1322 acres
- Business has grown by an average of 22% annually
- Received the prestigious Velvet Turf Award two years running

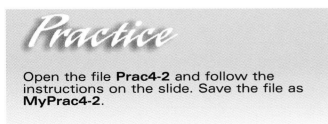

*Practice*

Open the file **Prac4-2** and follow the instructions on the slide. Save the file as **MyPrac4-2**.

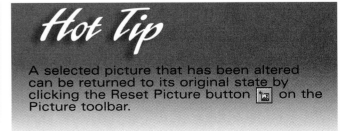

*Hot Tip*

A selected picture that has been altered can be returned to its original state by clicking the Reset Picture button on the Picture toolbar.

**PowerPoint 2000**

 # Inserting a Picture from a File

**Concept**

When adding graphics to a presentation, you are not limited to the clips found in the Insert Clip Art dialog box. If you are handy with image or drawing software, or if you have other art files available to you, you can insert your own pictures in a presentation.

**Do It!**

Trista wants to insert a picture she created with Windows 98's Paint program in one of her slides. Then she will crop the picture.

**1** Go to Slide 6 of GSU Presentation 4.

**2** Click Insert, highlight Picture, and then click From File. The Insert Picture dialog box will appear.

**3** Use the Look in: box to select the drive, folder, or other location that contains your Student Files folder. Double-click the folder in the dialog box's contents window to open the folder.

**4** Click the file named Check box to select it in the contents window. A preview of the picture will appear in the right half of the dialog box (see **Figure 4-9**).

**5** Click the Insert button . The dialog box closes and the Check box picture appears in the middle of the slide. The Picture toolbar will also appear.

**6** Click the Crop button on the Picture toolbar to activate the Crop tool.

**7** Place the mouse pointer over the sizing handle in the middle of the picture's right side. The pointer will change to the icon on the Crop button.

**8** Click the sizing handle with the Crop tool and drag to the left until the right border of the picture has completely cut off the text Check! (be careful not to cut off the top of the check mark). Then release the mouse button. The text portion of the picture disappears.

**9** Use the arrow keys on the keyboard to nudge the cropped picture so that it is centered on the slide and spaced evenly between Recently Acquired Accounts and Argyle County Municpal Stadium.

**10** Deselect the Crop tool and the picture and save your changes. Your slide should now look like the one shown in **Figure 4-10**.

**More**

PowerPoint allows you to insert a variety of image file formats into a presentation. Pictures made with the Paint program are bitmap files, represented by the file extension .bmp. The Clip Art files that come with PowerPoint are Windows metafiles, represented by the extension .wmf. In general, you can edit other image file types just like Clip Art, but there are some exceptions. For example, you would not be able to use the Recolor Picture feature on a bitmap.

Figure 4-9  Insert Picture dialog box

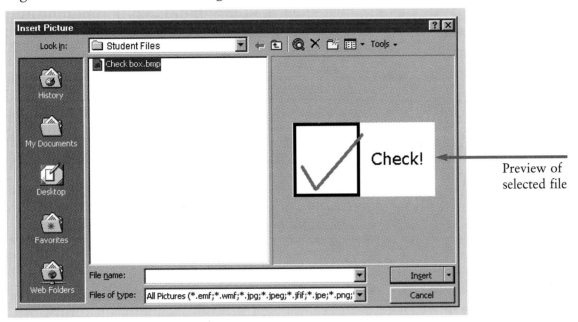

Preview of
selected file

Figure 4-10  Cropped picture inserted from file

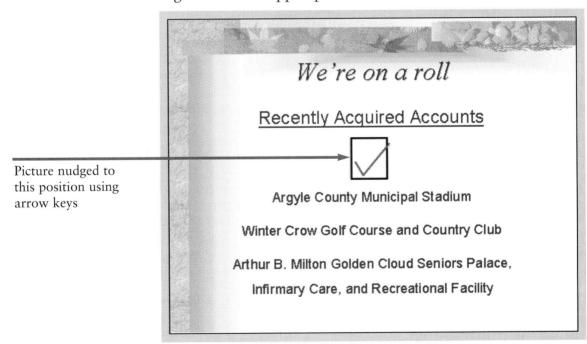

Picture nudged to
this position using
arrow keys

Create a one slide presentation and insert
the picture file **Prac4-3** from your Student
Files folder. Save the new presentation as
**MyPrac4-3**.

### Hot Tip

If you click on the arrow on the right edge
of the Insert button in the Insert Picture
dialog box, you can choose to link the picture you are inserting to its source file.
Then, any changes made to the source file
will also be reflected in the presentation.

 **Inserting a Chart**

## Concept

As you become more skilled at designing a presentation, you will discover that certain types of information are presented best through certain media. So far, the content of your presentation has used mostly text to express its key points. Some data, such as numbers and statistics, makes a greater impact on the viewer when it is displayed graphically as a chart. PowerPoint allows you to embed a chart in a slide, while still permitting you to alter its data and appearance.

## Do It!

Trista has gathered some data that compares Green Side Up favorably to several competitors. She would like to present this data as a chart on a new slide.

**1** With your presentation on Slide 6, click 🖼 to open the New Slide dialog box. Choose the Chart AutoLayout, which includes a placeholder for a chart, and title the new Slide 7 How our sod stacks up.

**2** Double-click the chart placeholder to launch Microsoft Graph 2000, a separate application used to create charts in Office 2000 files. A datasheet filled in with default data will appear over the slide, and a chart that corresponds to the default data will be embedded in the slide (see **Figure 4-11**). Graph 2000 inserts the default data so that the chart has structure until you enter your own data. The datasheet consists of rows, which are numbered, and columns, which are lettered. The point where a column and a row intersect is known as a cell. Cells are named by combining their column letter and row number. Thus, the first cell in the datasheet is named A1. The text entries in the cells in the left column and top row of the datasheet are data labels that describe the data that follows them to the right or below. The actual data that occupies a column or row is called a data series. A data series is represented in a chart by a data series marker, which is graphical object such as a bar, line, column, or pie piece.

**3** When the mouse pointer is over the datasheet, it changes to ✚, a pointer you may recognize if you have used Microsoft Excel. The active cell in a datasheet is indicated by a thick border around it, known as the cell pointer. You can change the active cell by clicking on a new cell, or by moving the cell pointer with the arrow keys on the keyboard.

**4** Click cell A2 to make it the active cell, as shown in **Figure 4-12**.

**5** Click outside the chart on Slide 7 to exit Microsoft Graph. Save your presentation.

## More

Inserting a chart does not require that you add a Chart AutoLayout slide to a presentation. You can add a chart to any slide by choosing the Chart command from the Insert menu, or by clicking the Insert Chart button 🖼 on the Standard toolbar. Both operations launch Graph 2000 as you did above by double-clicking the chart placeholder. You will notice that the Standard toolbar transforms whenever Graph 2000 is running to include buttons related to working with charts.

Figure 4-11  Inserting chart

Chart datasheet

Data series marker

Chart based on default data from datasheet

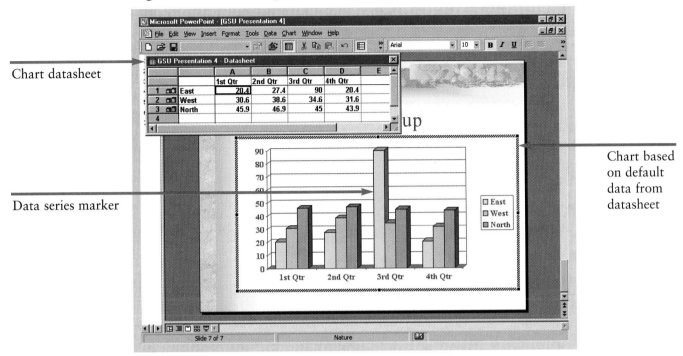

Figure 4-12  Default datasheet

Columns run vertically

Rows run horizontally

Data label

Cell D3

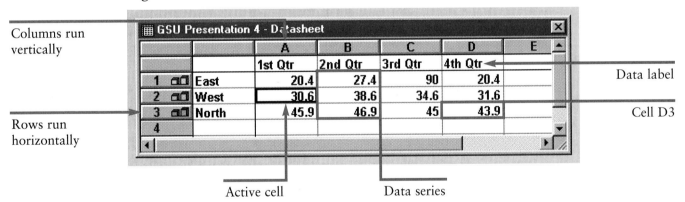

Active cell

Data series

Open file **Prac4-4** and follow the instructions on the slide. Save the file as **MyPrac4-4**.

*Hot Tip*

The standard PowerPoint menu commands will also be replaced by chart-related commands when Microsoft Graph 2000 is running.

# Customzing the Datasheet

## Concept

Once you have inserted a chart in a PowerPoint slide, you need to edit the datasheet so that the resulting chart reflects your own data and not the default data provided by application. Otherwise, your chart will have no significance to the presentation. The datasheet window is always available to you, so you can edit a chart as often as is necessary.

## Do It!

Trista will enter her comparison data in her chart's datasheet.

**1** Double-click the chart on Slide 7 to open Graph 2000 and the datasheet.

**2** Click the blank cell above the East data label and to the left of the 1st Qtr label.

**3** Type Sod Farms and then press [Enter] to confirm the data label and select the cell below it that contains the East data label.

**4** Type Green Side Up to replace the East label and press [Enter] again.

**5** Type Lawns by Larry to replace the West label, press [Enter], type Marquis de Sod to replace the North label, press [Enter], type Turfin' USA in the blank cell, and press [Tab].

**6** Click the cell that contains the 1st Qtr label to select it, replace the label with Acres Growing and then press [Tab]. Replace the 2nd Qtr label with Acres Installed Last Year and press [Tab] again.

**7** Right-click (click with the right mouse button) the selector button [ C ] at the top of column C, and then click the Delete command on the pop-up menu that appears. Repeat the process to delete the data that moved into column C when you deleted it the first time.

**8** Enter the following numbers to complete the datasheet:

| | |
|---|---|
| Cell A1: 1322 | Cell B1: 694 |
| Cell A2: 923 | Cell B2: 420 |
| Cell A3: 896 | Cell B3: 346 |
| Cell A4: 890 | Cell B4: 402 |

Your completed datasheet should now look like **Figure 4-13**.

**9** Click a blank area of the presentation window to close the datasheet and Graph 2000. The chart on Slide 7 will be updated with your data, shown in **Figure 4-14**.

**10** Save your presentation.

## More

When you are working in Graph 2000, you can point to any data series marker with the mouse pointer to receive a ScreenTip that summarizes the marker. For example, if you pointed to the first column, the ScreenTip would say Series "Green Side Up" Point "Acres Growing" Value: 1322.

Figure 4-13 Completed datasheet

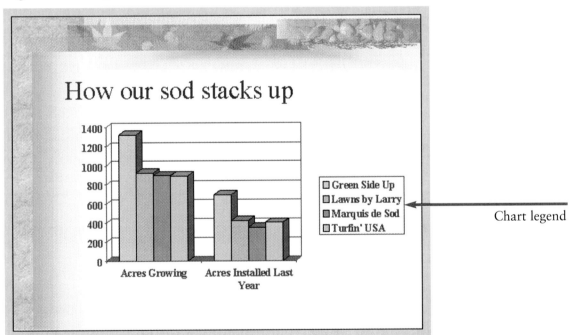

This data label is displayed fully because the cell to the right of it is empty; labels that are cut off will appear completely in the chart

Figure 4-14 Updated chart

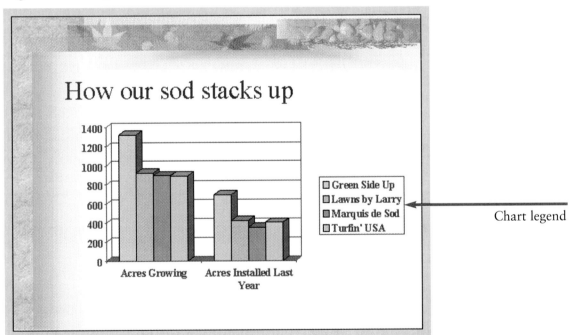

Chart legend

PowerPoint 2000

## Practice

Open the file **Prac4-5** and follow the instructions on the slide. Save the file as **MyPrac4-5**.

## Hot Tip

If you need to work with your chart's datasheet but it does not appear when you double-click the chart, click the View Datasheet button 📊 on the Standard toolbar.

# Changing a Chart's Type

## Concept

When you inserted a chart earlier in this lesson, PowerPoint's default choice for the type of chart was a Clustered Column chart with a 3-D visual effect. Even after you have finished a chart, you can still change its type. You may want to do this because you think another chart type will represent your data better, or simply because it interacts better with the other slide elements.

## Do It!

Trista wants to change her chart from Clustered Column to a Clustered Bar chart.

**1** Double-click the chart on Slide 7. Close the Datasheet window if it appears.

**2** Click Chart on the menu bar, and then click the Chart Type command. The Chart Type dialog box will open to its Standard Types tab. The Chart type: scrolling list box displays the basic chart types you can use in PowerPoint. The Chart sub-type: section to the right of this list box displays the sub-types available for the chart type that is selected in the list box. The sub-type highlighted in black is the one that is currently in use.

**3** Click Bar in the list of chart types to select it and display its sub-types. The first sub-type, Clustered Bar, will be selected automatically.

**4** Click the sub-type directly below Clustered Bar to select it. Its description, which appears below the sub-types, should read Clustered bar with a 3-D visual effect, as shown in **Figure 4-15**.

**5** Click ⬛ OK to close the dialog box and change the chart type. Deselect the chart, which should look like the one shown in **Figure 4-16**, and save your changes.

## More

Table 4-1  Common chart types

| CHART TYPE | DESCRIPTION | EXAMPLE |
|---|---|---|
| 📊 Column | Data changes over time or quantitative comparisons among items | Quarterly income projections |
| 📊 Bar | Similar to a column chart, but horizontal orientation places more value on the X value | Individual sales performance |
| 📈 Line | Trends in data at fixed intervals | Tracking stock trends |
| 🥧 Pie | The percentage each value contributes to the whole. Used for a single data series | Budgets, chief exports of a country |
| 📉 XY (Scatter) | Comparative relationships between seemingly dissimilar data | Scientific data analysis |
| 📄 Surface | The range of intersections between two sets of data | Optimal fuel consumption |

Figure 4-15  Chart Type dialog box

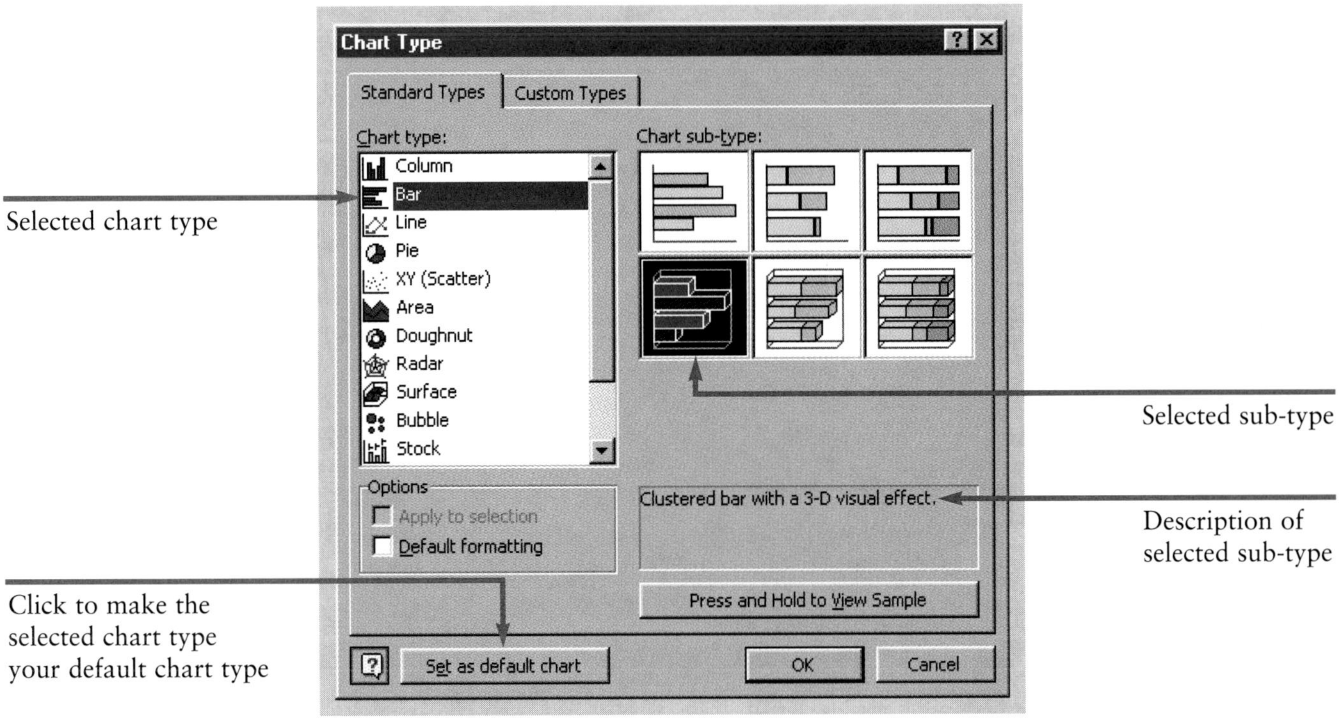

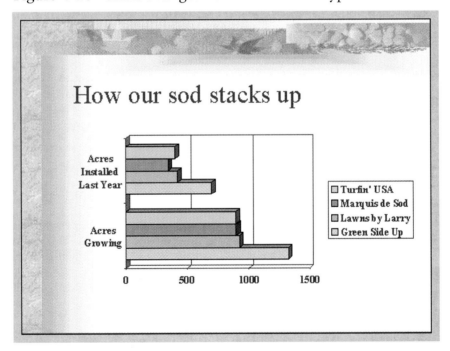

Selected chart type

Selected sub-type

Description of selected sub-type

Click to make the selected chart type your default chart type

Figure 4-16  Chart changed to Clustered Bar type

*Practice*

Open **MyPrac4-5** and change the chart on Slide 2 to a Line chart. Save the file as **MyPrac4-6**.

*Hot Tip*

Click and hold the long button labeled **Press and Hold to View Sample** in the Chart Type dialog box to preview your chart with its new type without changing the actual chart.

**PowerPoint 2000**

# Setting Chart Options

## Concept

A chart can be made up of numerous components including a legend, titles, axes, gridlines, and data labels. The Chart Options dialog box allows you to determine how and where these items will appear, or if they will appear at all.

## Do It!

Trista has decided to give her chart a title and reposition the chart's legend.

1. Double-click the chart on Slide 7 and close the datasheet.

2. Click Chart on the menu bar, then click Chart Options. The Chart Options dialog box opens. The dialog box contains six tabs, each of which allow you to control certain aspects of a chart. Each tab also includes a preview of the chart that reflects your changes as soon as you make them.

3. If not already in front, click the Titles tab to bring it to the front of the dialog box. Then click in the text box labeled Chart title: to place the insertion point there.

4. Type Growth Comparison for Industry Leaders. The title will appear in the text box and in the preview, as shown in **Figure 4-17**. Do not worry if the preview appears crowded as the actual chart will be displayed correctly.

5. Click the Legend tab to activate it.

6. The Placement option for the legend is currently set to Right. Click the radio button labeled Top to move the legend above the chart.

7. Click [ OK ] to accept the settings you have changed. The new Chart Options are shown on the deselected chart in **Figure 4-18**.

8. Save the changes you have made to the presentation.

## More

After you alter Chart Options, you may need to adjust the size of the chart to accommodate items that you have moved or added. You can do this without working in Graph 2000. If you click on a chart once, it will be selected just like a text box or other object you have inserted. You will then be able to resize the chart by dragging one of its eight sizing handles. You may also reposition the entire chart by dragging it from its center.

Figure 4-17  Chart Options dialog box

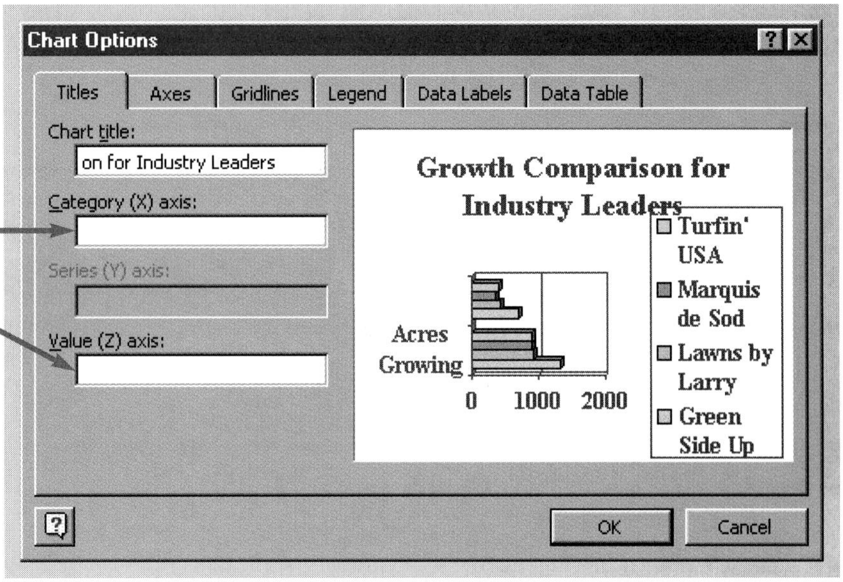

Use these text boxes to
title individual axes

Figure 4-18  Chart new options

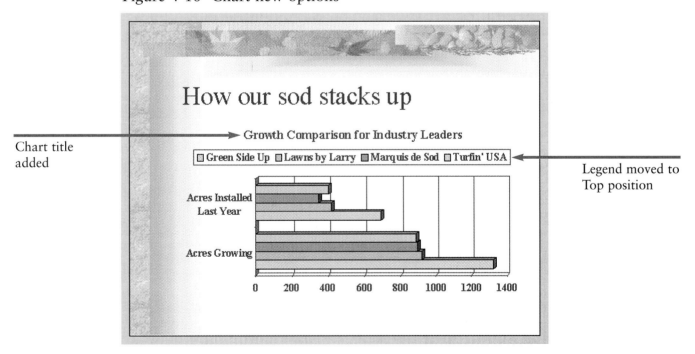

Chart title
added

Legend moved to
Top position

*Practice*

Open **MyPrac4-6**. Add the title **MyPrac4-7**
to the chart on Slide 2 and move the
chart's legend to the left of the chart. Save
the file as **MyPrac4-7**.

*Hot Tip*

A legend is not required for every chart. To
remove the legend from a chart, remove
the check from the **Show legend** check
box on the Legend tab in the Chart Options
dialog box.

 # Formatting Chart Elements

## Concept

Now that you have learned how to convert a chart to a completely different type and modify its general structure, it is time to learn how to improve your chart by working with individual elements. You can modify many aspects of a chart including its text, colors, textures, and organization. Though the chart can be selected as a single entity, each of its components can also be selected and formatted individually. This flexibility permits you to enhance the overall appearance of the chart and call attention to specific data.

## Do It!

Trista wants to italicize and change the color and font of her Category Axis labels, increase her chart depth, and add texture to one of her data series markers.

**1** Double-click the chart to open Graph 2000. You do not need to view the datasheet.

**2** Click the Category Axis label Acres Installed Last Year on the chart to select the entire Category Axis.

**3** Click 𝐼 on the Formatting toolbar to italicize the two Category Axis labels.

**4** Click Format on the menu bar, and then click Selected Axis. The Format Axis dialog box appears.

**5** Click the Font tab to bring it to the front of the dialog box. Notice that Bold Italic is selected in the Font style: list box, as shown in Figure 4-19. The Bold style formatting was applied automatically when you created the chart.

**6** Click the drop-down arrow on the right end of the Color: box, which currently says Automatic. A color palette will open.

**7** Click the Red color square at the beginning of the third row of the palette.

**8** Click OK to close the dialog box and make the color change.

**9** With the Category Axis still selected, use the Formatting toolbar's Font box to change the font from Times New Roman to Arial. The Category Axis labels should be formatted like those shown in Figure 4-20.

**10** Click one of the two horizonatal bars that represent Green Side Up's data in the chart. Both Green Side Up data series markers will be selected.

**11** Click Format, then click Selected Data Series. The Format Data Series dialog box will appear.

**12** Click the Options tab to bring it to the front of the dialog box, as shown in Figure 4-21.

Figure 4-19 Font tab of Format Axis dialog box

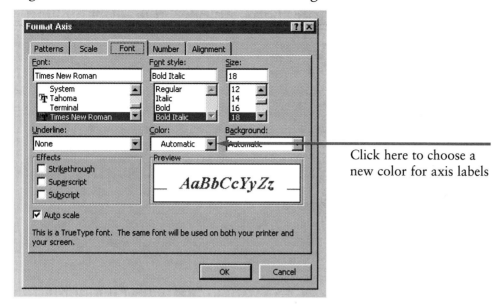

Click here to choose a
new color for axis labels

Figure 4-20 Font tab of Format Axis dialog box

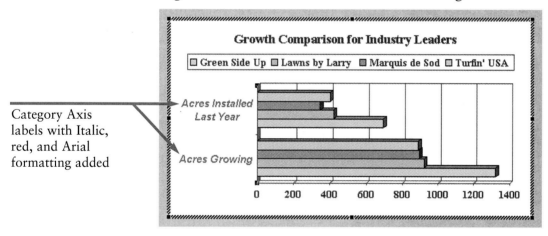

Category Axis
labels with Italic,
red, and Arial
formatting added

Figure 4-21 Format Data Series dialog box

Sets distance between data
markers in a 3-D chart

Sets distance between data
categories in chart

Sets depth of chart relative
to its width

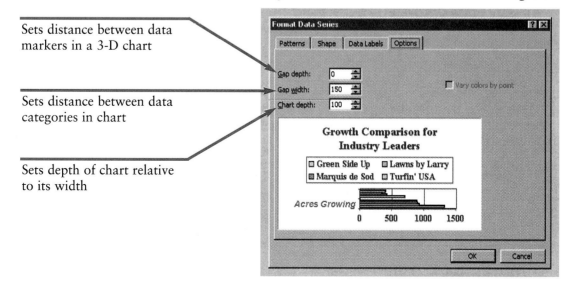

# Formatting Chart Elements (continued)

**Do It!**

**13** Double-click inside the Chart depth: box to select its current value. Type 1000 to replace the value with a new one.

**14** Click ⬚ OK ⬚ to close the dialog box and confirm the depth change. Your chart should resemble **Figure 4-22**. Notice that even though only one data series marker was selected, this option affects all of the data series markers.

**15** With the Green Side Up data series still selected, click the Format Data Series button 📇 on the Standard toolbar. The Format Data Series dialog box should open to the Patterns tab.

**16** Click the Fill Effects button ⬚ Fill Effects... ⬚ the bottom of the Patterns tab's **Area** section. The Fill Effects dialog box appears.

**17** Click the Texture tab to bring it to the front of the dialog box. The Texture tab offers a number of premade textures that you can apply to a chart object. When you click on a texture to select it, its name will appear below the Texture: box. You can also apply your own texture if you have an image file available.

**18** Click the Other Texture button ⬚ Other Texture... ⬚ to apply your own texture. This opens the Select Texture dialog box, which is very similar to the Open dialog box you would use to open a PowerPoint file.

**19** Use the Look in: box and the contents window to find the file **Doit 4-8,** which is a grass texture image file, in your Student Files folder. When you locate the file, double-click it in the contents window. The Select Texture dialog box will close, and the grass texture will be added to the Texture: box and be selected, as shown in **Figure 4-23**.

**20** Click ⬚ OK ⬚ to close the Fill Effects dialog box. Then click ⬚ OK ⬚ to close the Format Data Series dialog box. The grass texture will be added to the Green Side Up data series markers (see **Figure 4-24**).

**21** Deselect the chart and save your changes.

**More**

3-D charts have special formatting options available that you can access by choosing the 3-D View command from the Chart menu. The 3-D View dialog box allows you to change the elevation of the chart so that is viewed from a different angle. You can also rotate a chart clockwise or counter-clockwise, which has a different effect depending on your chart type. Other more general formatting options are available on the toolbars when you are working in Graph 2000. Some of these are highlighted in **Table 4-3**, which can be found on page PP 4.32.

Figure 4-22  Chart with depth change

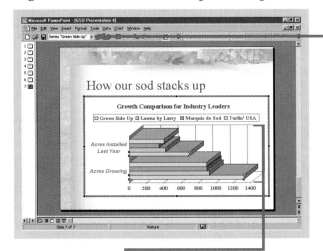

Use Chart Objects drop-down list to select any
chart object from the Standard toolbar

Depth change affects
all data series markers

Figure 4-23  New texture added

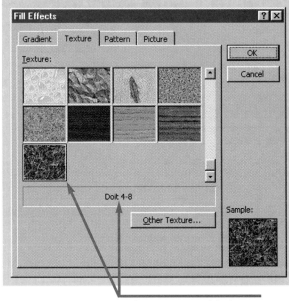

File Doit 4-8 added to
Texture tab and selected

Figure 4-24  Texture applied to data series marker

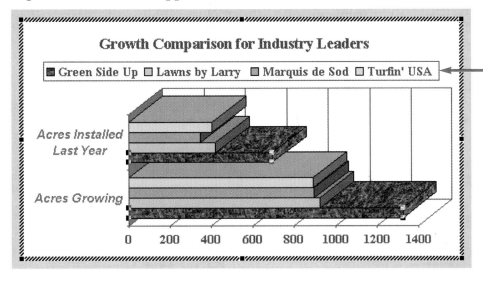

New texture also appears
in chart legend

*Practice*

Open the file **Prac4-8** and follow the
instructions on the slide. Save the file as
**MyPrac4-8**.

*Hot Tip*

You can open a formatting related dialog
box for any chart object by simply double-
clicking the object.

 # Adding Transition Effects

## Concept

After you have constructed your slides, it is time to think about the manner in which you will present them. Adding slide transition effects adds visual interest and emphasis to your presentation. Unlike a traditional slide show, PowerPoint's capabilities allow you to set controls that determine how a slide is displayed on the screen after the previous one is shown. You can set slides to move off the screen in different directions, to appear as if they are fading into or out of view, or even to dissolve into one another.

## Do It!

Trista will now add transition effects to her presentation slides.

**1** Click the Slide Sorter View button 🔳. The presentation will be displayed in Slide Sorter view, which displays miniature versions of the presentation's seven slides. The slide you were viewing when you switched to Slide Sorter View will be selected (indicated by a heavy, blue border), and the **Slide Sorter** toolbar will appear (see **Figure 4-25**).

**2** Click Slide 1 to select it if it is not already selected.

**3** Click Slide Show on the menu bar, then select **Slide Transition** from the menu. The Slide Transition dialog box will open.

**4** To select an effect, click the **Effect** drop-down list arrow to produce a list of available effects.

**5** Scroll down until **Uncover Up** is visible in the list.

**6** Click Uncover Up. It will appear in the Effect list box (see **Figure 4-26**) and a preview of the effect will run in the dialog box.

**7** Click the Slow radio button to set the transition speed. A second preview of the transition effect will be shown at the new speed.

Figure 4-25  GSU Presentation 4 in Slide Sorter View

Slide Sorter
toolbar

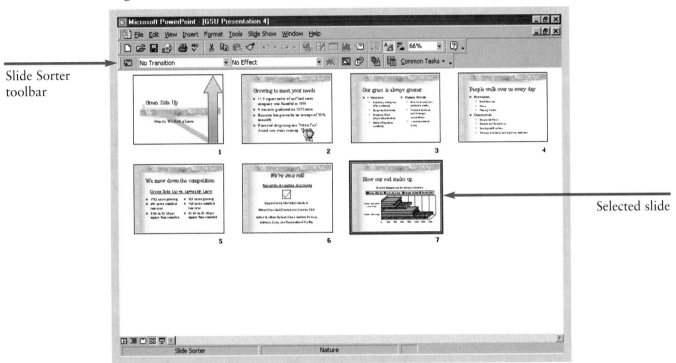

Selected slide

Figure 4-26  Slide Transition dialog box

Preview of selected
effects shown here

Use radio buttons to
set transition speed

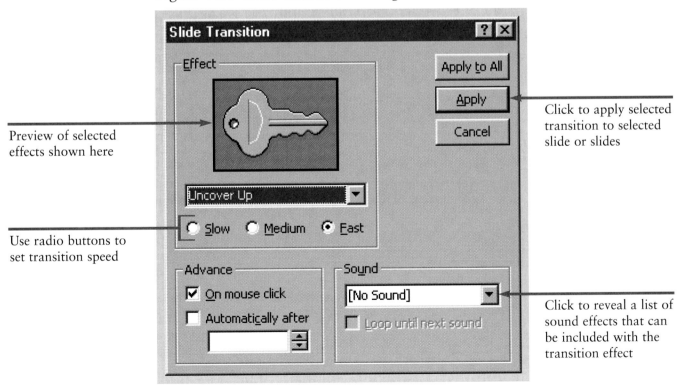

Click to apply selected
transition to selected
slide or slides

Click to reveal a list of
sound effects that can
be included with the
transition effect

# Adding Transition Effects (continued)

## Do It!

**8** Click the On mouse click check box in the Advance section of the dialog box to clear it. Later in the lesson you will learn how to set automatic transition timings. Click [Apply to All]. The Transition Effects dialog box will close and the selected settings will be applied to every one of the slides in the presentation. A transition effect icon 🖅 will be displayed below each slide indicating that a transition effect has been applied.

**9** Click the Slide Transition Effects drop-down arrow on the Slide Sorter toolbar, then select Fade Through Black from the drop-down list. A preview of the effect will be displayed on Slide 1. Applying transitions in this way affects only the selected slide, not the whole presentation.

**10** Select Slide 3 and use the Slide Transition Effects drop-down list to apply the Wipe Down transition effect to it.

**11** Similarly apply the Dissolve effect to Slide 7. Your Slide Sorter window should look like the one shown in **Figure 4-27**.

**12** Save the changes you have made to your file.

## More

The Slide Transition dialog box can also be accessed by clicking the Slide Transition button 🖅 at the left end of the Slide Sorter toolbar, shown in **Figure 4-28**. This dialog box can only be opened if a slide is selected, even if you wish to apply a transition effect to all of the slides in a presentation. By clicking the Apply button rather than the Apply to All button, you can apply a transition effect to just the selected slide via this dialog box.

The Advance section of the Transition Effects dialog box lets you set the amount of time that passes before the next slide is automatically displayed. If the On mouse click box is checked, then clicking the left mouse button will advance the show.

Transitions may also have a sound associated with them. By choosing a sound in the Sound drop-down list the sound will automatically play when the transition is made. Selecting Other sound allows you to use any sound file you have available, provided it is in a file format that PowerPoint can play.

Figure 4-27 Sildes with transition effects

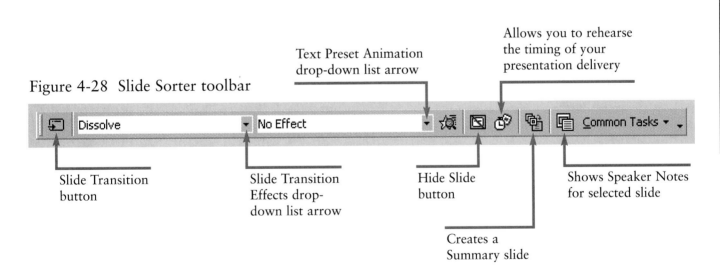

Transition effect applied to selected slide

Slide number

Transition effect icon

Figure 4-28 Slide Sorter toolbar

Text Preset Animation drop-down list arrow

Allows you to rehearse the timing of your presentation delivery

Slide Transition button

Slide Transition Effects drop-down list arrow

Hide Slide button

Shows Speaker Notes for selected slide

Creates a Summary slide

*Practice*

Open file **Prac4-9**. Apply the following transiton effects: Slide 1 – Wipe Left, Slow; Slide 2 – Checkerboard Across, Medium; Slide 3 – Cover Right, Slow. Save the file as **MyPrac4-9**.

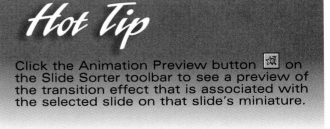

*Hot Tip*

Click the Animation Preview button 🔲 on the Slide Sorter toolbar to see a preview of the transition effect that is associated with the selected slide on that slide's miniature.

PowerPoint 2000

# Timing Slide Transitions

## Concept

PowerPoint allows you to control the amount of time a slide spends on the screen before the next one appears during a slide show. Some slides require more time for the audience to absorb and for the presenter to explain, and therefore need more screen time.

## Do It!

Based on the content of each slide, Trista would like to set the appropriate slide transition timings.

**1** Click Slide 1 to select it in Slide Sorter View.

**2** Click Slide Show on the menu bar, then click Slide Transition. The Slide Transition dialog box will open with the transition effect you selected in the previous Skill, Fade Through Black, selected.

**3** Click the Automatically after check box in the Advance section of the dialog box to activate it. The default value, 00:00, will appear selected in the time text box.

**4** Enter 5 to replace the 00:00 in the time text box (**Figure 4-29**), then click [ Apply ]. The dialog box closes and you will be returned to Slide Sorter View. The number you entered is recognized as representing seconds. Notice that Slide 1 now has :05 below it indicating that it will advance automatically after five seconds.

**5** Click Slide 2 to select it. Then hold down [Ctrl] on the keyboard and click Slide 4, Slide 5, and Slide 6, to add them to the selection.

**6** The four selected slides all have the Uncover Up transition effect applied to them. Return to the Slide Transition dialog box and set these four slides to advance automatically after 15 seconds (remember to use the Apply button and not the Apply to All button).

**7** Set Slide 3 to advance automatically after 12 seconds and Slide 7 after 10 seconds. Your Slide Sorter View should now look like **Figure 4-30**.

**8** Click Slide 1 to select it, then click the Slide Show button 🖵. The slide show begins at the selected slide and runs until the last slide is shown, after which you can return to Slide Sorter View by clicking the mouse button. When you have finished watching the slide show, save the presentation.

## More

When setting transition times, it is important to consider what is shown on each slide. A brief slide, such as the opening slide of Trista's presentation, does not need nearly as much time on the screen as her third slide, which contains much more information. Sounds, movies, complex animations, and other slide elements all add to the amount of time necessary for the audience to view the slide and comprehend the message that you are trying to convey. It is also necessary to take the length of the presenter's explanation, including speaker's notes, into account. If the presenter's accompanying notes are lengthy, it may be a better idea to advance a slide manually with the mouse, which will allow much more flexibility when presenting.

Figure 4-29  Setting slide timings

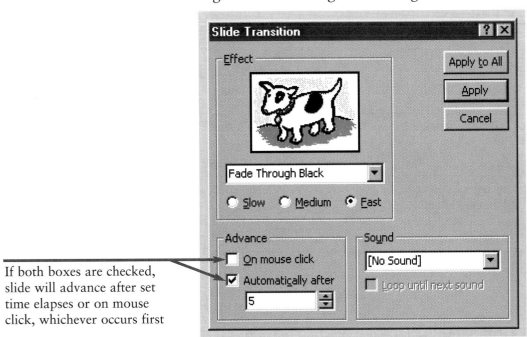

If both boxes are checked, slide will advance after set time elapses or on mouse click, whichever occurs first

Figure 4-30  Slides with transition effects

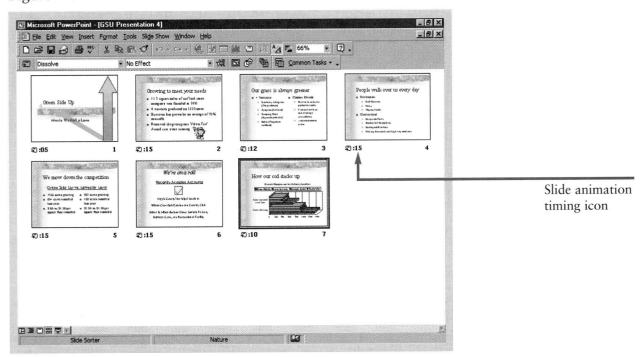

Slide animation timing icon

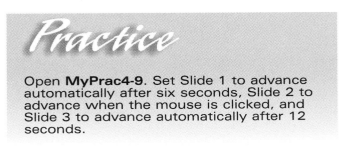

Practice

Open **MyPrac4-9**. Set Slide 1 to advance automatically after six seconds, Slide 2 to advance when the mouse is clicked, and Slide 3 to advance automatically after 12 seconds.

Hot Tip

If you do not wish to display a selected slide during a presentation, you can hide it by using the **Hide Slide** button on the Slide Sorter toolbar. A gray box with a line through it will appear over the slide's number.

# Annotating Slides

## Concept

There are times when you might want to halt the slide show in order to explain a specific point that your a trying to make further. PowerPoint has a pen feature that allows you to draw on or annotate your slides. You can even pause your presentation to allow for more time to explain your annotations without worrying about being cut off by the next slide transition.

## Do It!

Trista wants to highlight data on Slide 5 of her presentation.

1. Click Slide Show, then click Set Up Show. The Set Up Show dialog box will open, as shown in **Figure 4-31**.

2. Click the Pen color: drop-down list arrow. The Pen color palette will appear.

3. Click the sixth color square from the left (its ScreenTip will read Follow Accent Scheme Color). The Pen color palette closes and the selected color appears in the Pen color: box.

4. Click OK to close the dialog box. Then, select Slide 5 and click 🖳 to begin a slide show on Slide 5.

5. When the slide show starts, move the mouse. A transparent icon will appear in the lower-left corner of the slide.

6. Click the Slide Show pop-up menu icon 📖◣, highlight the Pointer Options command, and then select Pen from the submenu. The pointer will change from the standard arrow to the annotation pen pointer ◣.

7. Circle the two numbers that represent the number of acres growing by clicking and dragging around them with the annotation pointer. The numbers will be circled in the color you chose in step 3. Your screen should resemble **Figure 4-32**.

8. Click 📖◣ again, and this time highlight the the Screen command on the pop-up menu, and then click the Pause command on the submenu. The presentation is now paused and will not advance to the next slide.

9. Use the Pointer Options command to switch back to the standard arrow pointer, and then use the Screen command to resume your slide show.

## More

When the annotation pen pointer is active your slide show will not advance, allowing you to write or draw without interruption. Selecting Arrow from the slide show Pointer Options submenu will cause the mouse pointer to revert to an arrow, and allow the slide show to proceed if it is not on Pause. Or, you can move to another slide by selecting Previous or Next from the slide show pop-up menu, which will take you out of annotation mode and return you to the slide show at the requested point. Markings that you make with the annotation pen are not permanent and are erased as soon as another slide is displayed or the show is ended. Alternatively, pressing [E] erases all annotations without having to leave the present slide.

Figure 4-31  Set Up Show dialog box

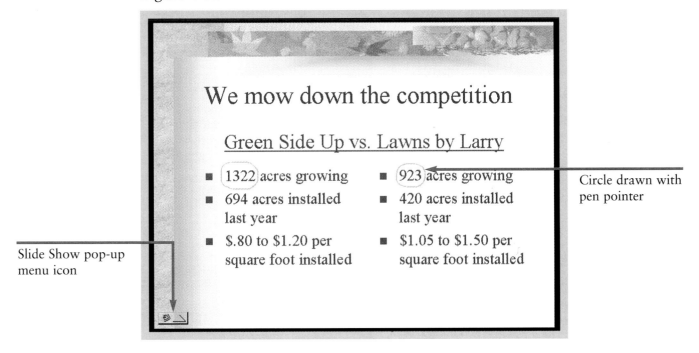

Allows you to specify which slides will appear in a slide show

Click to allow presentation to run repeatedly

Pen color drop-down list arrow

Allows you to advance slides with mouse

Figure 4-32  Annotated slide

Circle drawn with pen pointer

Slide Show pop-up menu icon

PowerPoint 2000

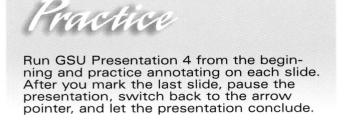

*Practice*

Run GSU Presentation 4 from the beginning and practice annotating on each slide. After you mark the last slide, pause the presentation, switch back to the arrow pointer, and let the presentation conclude.

*Hot Tip*

To make perfect vertical or horizontal lines while using the annotation pen, press **[Shift]** while drawing. Release [Shift] to add curves again. Alternating between straight and curved lines in this way will make your drawings appear more precise.

# Navigating During a Slide Show

**Concept**

While slide presentations generally follow a sequential order, occasions may arise when you want to display slides out of order. PowerPoint provides several ways to show any of your presentation's slides at any point during a slide show without having to end the show and restart it.

**Do It!**

Trista would like to explore PowerPoint's Slide Show navigation capabilities.

1. Run a Slide Show of GSU Presentation 4 starting on Slide 2.

2. When the presentation starts, right-click anywhere on the slide to open the Slide Show pop-up menu (this is the same menu that opens when you click the Slide Show pop-up menu icon).

3. Highlight the Go command on the pop-up menu, and then click the **Slide Navigator** command on the Go submenu. The Slide Navigator dialog box appear, as shown in **Figure 4-33**.

4. Click 7. **How our sod stacks up** to select Slide 7, and then click ▢ Go To ▢. The slide show resumes, starting on Slide 7.

5. Right-click Slide 7 to open the pop-up menu again.

6. Highlight the Go command, and then highlight the **By Title** command on the Go submenu. A second submenu, consisting of all your slide titles and the Slide Navigator command, will appear as shown in **Figure 4-34**. A check mark precedes the current slide.

7. Click **1 Green Side Up** on the By Title submenu to go to Slide 1. Allow the slide show to run through to the end.

**More**

Table 4-2  Slide Show keyboard commands

| KEY | FUNCTION |
| --- | --- |
| [H] | Advances to the next hidden slide |
| [B] or [W] | Displays a blank black or white screen |
| [→], [N], [Enter], or [Space] | Advances to the next animation effect or slide |
| [←], [P], or [Back Space] | Goes to the previous animation effect or slide |
| [*Slide Number*] + [Enter] | Goes to a specific slide |
| [S] | Pauses a slide show or restarts a paused slide show |
| [Esc] | Exits the slide show |

Figure 4-33 Slide Navigator dialog box

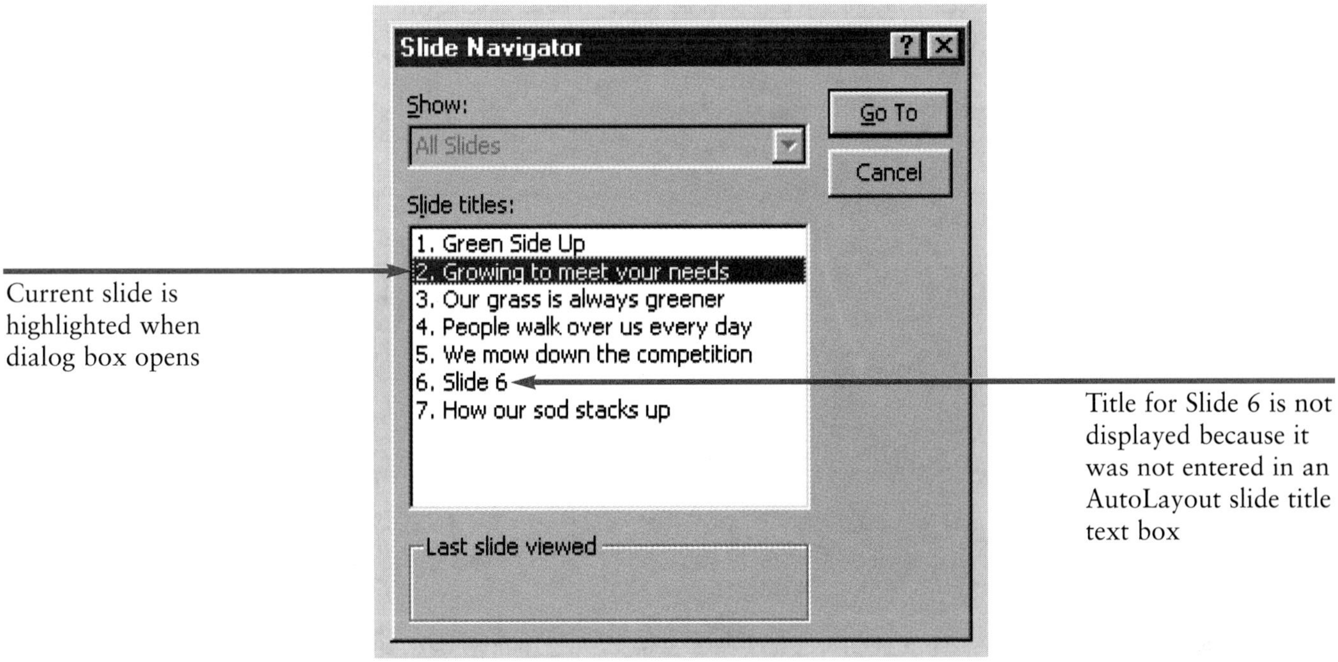

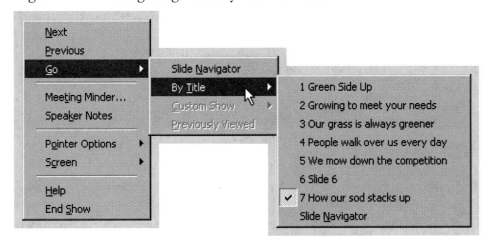

Current slide is highlighted when dialog box opens

Title for Slide 6 is not displayed because it was not entered in an AutoLayout slide title text box

Figure 4-34 Navigating with By Title submenu

PowerPoint 2000

**Practice**

Open **Prac4-12** and start a slide show on Slide 5. Open the Slide Navigator and go to Slide 8. Then use the By Title command to go to Slide 1. Exit the slide show and close the file without saving changes.

**Hot Tip**

Pressing [F1] during a slide show or clicking the Help command on the Slide Show pop-up menu displays a comprehensive list of slide show controls.

| Function | Button/Mouse | Menu | Keyboard |
|---|---|---|---|
| Insert Clip Art | 🖼 | Click Insert, then highlight Picture, then click Clip Art | |
| Format data series (or other selected chart object) | 🖼 | Click Format, then click Selected Data Series (or other object) | [Ctrl]+[1] |
| Run slide show | 🖥 | Click Slide Show, then click View Show | [F5] |
| Get help during slide show/view keyboard shortcuts | Right-click, then click Help on pop-up menu | | [F1] |
| End slide show | Right-click, then click End Show | | [Esc] |

**Table 4-3  Graph 2000 formatting tools**

| BUTTON | COMMAND | FUNCTION |
|---|---|---|
| 👆 | Import File | Opens the Import File dialog box, allowing you to import a file, an entire sheet of data, or a selected range into a chart |
| ▦ | View Datasheet | Displays the datasheet window, or hides it if it is currently showing |
| ▤ or ▥ | By Row or By Column | Plots chart data series from data across rows or down columns |
| ▦ | Data Table | Displays the values for each data series in a grid below the chart |
| ▥ or ▤ | Category Axis Gridlines or Value Axis Gridlines | Shows or hides category axis or value axis gridlines in charts |
| ✎ or ✎ | Angle Text Downward or Angle Text Upward | Rotates selected text down or up at a 45-degree angle to more efficiently utilize the available space on a chart |

# Identify Key Features

Name the items identified by callouts in the figures below.

Figure 4-35  Elements of Slide Sorter View

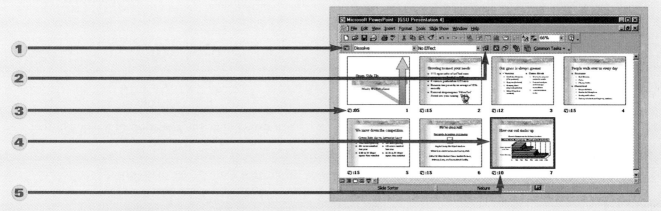

Figure 4-36  Elements of Graph 2000

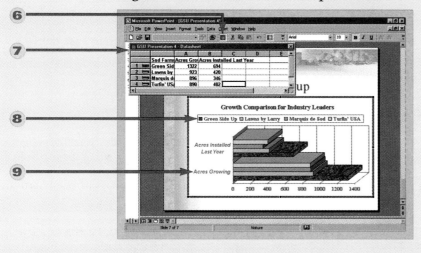

# Select The Best Answer

10. Provides pictures that you can add to your presentation

11. Allows you to mark a slide temporarily during a slide show

12. Controls the manner in which slides appear on the screen

13. An example of a slide transition effect

14. Stores the information that drives a chart in tabular form

15. The intersection of a column and a row

16. Allows you to jump to any slide during the delivery of a presentation

17. Includes the Pointer Options command

a. Cell

b. Wipe Down

c. Slide Navigator

d. Insert Clip Art dialog box

e. Slide Show pop-up menu

f. Pen pointer

g. Datasheet

h. Slide Transition dialog box

## Complete the Statement

18. You can add texture to a chart object using an option on the:

    a. Patterns tab

    b. Fill Effects tab

    d. Font tab

    e. Chart toolbar

19. You can edit and format Clip Art by using the:

    a. Standard toolbar

    b. Picture toolbar

    c. Microsoft Clip Gallery

    d. Slide Navigator

20. A column is an example of a:

    a. Data series marker

    b. Data label

    c. Category axis

    d. Value axis

21. When working in a datasheet, pressing [Enter] moves the cell pointer:

    a. One cell to the right

    b. One cell to the left

    c. To the next row in the same column

    d. To the next column in the same row

22. Chart titles and legends can be added in the:

    a. Chart Type dialog box

    b. Notes pane

    c. Datasheet window

    d. Chart Options dialog box

23. Adding transition effects and slide timings is best accomplished in:

    a. Normal View

    b. Slide Sorter View

    c. Microsoft Graph 2000

    d. Slide Show mode

24. You can change the elevation of a chart in the:

    a. Chart Options dialog box

    b. Format Data Series dialog box

    c. 3-D View dialog box

    d. Presentation window

25. To change a Bar chart to a Pie chart, use the:

    a. Chart Options dialog box

    b. Formatting toolbar

    c. Datasheet

    d. Chart Type command

26. To maintain precise control over your presentation, set your slides to advance:

    a. Automatically

    b. Automatically after 10 seconds

    c. On mouse click

    d. With sound effects

# *Interactivity*

## *Test Your Skills*

1. Insert pictures into a slide:

   a. Open the PowerPoint file **TYS4-1** from your Student Files folder.

   b. Insert the Clip Art file named **summer** into the Title Slide.

   c. Resize and reposition the image so that it fits between the slide's subtitle and the dotted line below it.

   d. Insert the picture file named **TYS4 Image** from your Student Files folder.

   e. Position the image above the title text and resize it so that it covers most of the top of the slide.

2. Format a picture:

   a. Select the summer Clip Art picture you added in step 1 and activate the Picture toolbar.

   b. Open the Recolor Picture dialog box.

   c. Replace the color black with the color whose ScreenTip is **Follow Shadows Scheme Color**.

3. Add a chart to a presentation and format it:

   a. Start a new blank presentation. Make the first slide a **Title Only** slide.

   b. Insert a chart. You will be using the dummy data that appears in the datasheet.

   c. Close the Datasheet window, then drag the chart's border down so that it does not obscure the title box.

   d. Add the title **Accounts Acquired by Region** to the slide.

   e. Move the chart's legend to the left side.

   f. Create another title slide.

   g. Insert another chart. This time, delete rows 2 and 3 (West and North) from the datasheet.

   h. Close the datasheet.

   i. Change the chart type to **Exploded pie with a 3-D visual effect**.

   j. Title the slide **East Accounts by Quarter**.

   k. Create similar slides with charts for the West and North data. Make the West chart a plain pie chart, and the North chart a Doughnut chart.

   l. Select a data series from the doughnut chart and add texture to it.

   m. **Underline** the titles of each chart you created.

   n. Save the presentation as **Accounts**.

PowerPoint 2000

# Interactivity (continued)

4. Add transition effects and advance timings to a presentation:

   a. Open the PowerPoint file **TYS4-4** from your Student Files folder.

   b. Apply the **Box In** transition effect at **Slow** speed to Slide 1, and set it to advance automatically after five seconds.

   c. Apply the **Horizontal Blinds** transition effect at **Medium** speed to Slide 2, and set it to advance after 10 seconds.

   d. Use the Slide Sorter toolbar to apply the **Random Bars Vertical** transition effect to Slide 3. Then set the slide to advance when you click the mouse.

5. Practice running a slide show:

   a. Run a slide show for TYS4-4 that starts on Slide 2.

   b. When you get to Slide 3, use the Pen pointer to underline the word **Congratulations!** on the screen.

   c. Use the **Slide Navigator** to go to Slide 1.

   d. Use the **By Title** command to go back to Slide 3.

---

## Problem Solving

1. Open the file **Solved3-1.ppt**, which is the brochure you created at the end of Lesson 3 for the country inn you are planning to open. Use PowerPoint's gallery of Clip Art to enliven the brochure. Each slide in the brochure should contain at least one example of Clip Art. Recolor the Clip Art pictures you add so that they match the Template Design scheme used in the presentation. Add a new slide to the presentation that compares your projected rates to those of other local inns in the form of a chart. Save the presentation as **Solved4-1.ppt**.

2. Using the PowerPoint skills you have learned, create a five slide comic strip using Clip Art pictures for your characters. The first slide should serve as an introductory panel that shows the comic strip's name and introduces the characters. Use the other four slides for the actual strip dialogue. Program this presentation so that each slide advances after 20 seconds or on a mouse click, whichever comes first. Also use exciting transition effects, appropriate for a comic. Save the presentation as **Solved4-2.ppt**.

3. Create a new blank presentation. On a Title Only slide, insert a chart. Edit the datasheet so that the chart will display the name of each of the four Lessons you have completed in this book, and the number of Skills each lesson contains. Once the chart is created, change it to a Pie chart. Format the pie slices so that one is black, one is red, one is blue, and one has texture. Place the chart's legend at the bottom of the chart. Save the file as **Solved4-3.ppt**.

4. Your consulting firm has been hired by large market all-news radio station to perform a demographic study of its listeners. You will be presenting your findings with PowerPoint. The data you have found (fictional) should be presented both as text and in chart form. Your study includes the following: separate breakdowns of the total audience by age group and gender; average number of hours listening per week, overall satisfaction with station's performance. Each of these statistical areas and the methods used to gather their data should be explained thoroughly in the presentation. Your work should also make full use of a Design Template, Clip Art, AutoShapes, slide transitions, slide timings, and all types of formatting. Save the finished project as **Solved4-4.ppt**.

# A

**Active cell**
The selected cell in a chart datasheet.

**Adjustment handle**
A small yellow diamond that appears when certain objects are selected. Dragging the handle allows you to alter the shape of the object.

**Annotation pen pointer**
A tool that enables you to draw freely on slides during a slide show.

**Answer Wizard tab**
PowerPoint help tab that replicates the Office Assistant by allowing you to ask questions or enter search topics in your own words.

**Application**
A software program that performs specific tasks, such as Microsoft PowerPoint.

**AutoContent Wizard**
A feature that assists you in designing a PowerPoint presentation quickly and easily. The AutoContent Wizard guides you through the steps of choosing basic layout design, style, and output type.

**AutoCorrect**
A feature that corrects common typing errors automatically as you type. AutoCorrect can be customized to correct specific mistakes that you frequently make.

**AutoLayout**
Any of 24 predesigned slides set up to accommodate different combinations of text, pictures, charts, and other objects.

**AutoShape**
One of numerous figures that can be drawn by simply selecting a shape from the Drawing toolbar and dragging the mouse. The user determines the dimensions and the location of an AutoShape.

# B

**Black and White View**
Shows how your presentation will appear when printed in black and white in case you do not have a color printer.

**Bullet**
A small graphic, usually a round or square dot, that is commonly used to designate items in a list.

# C

**Cell**
The basic unit of a datasheet where you enter data, formed by the intersection of a row and a column.

**Chart**
A graphical representation of data.

**Chart elements**
The objects that represent information in a chart such as bars, columns, or text labels.

**Chart type**
Determines the style in which a chart graphically interprets data.

**Click**
To press and release a mouse button in one motion; usually refers to the left mouse button.

**Clip Art**
Predrawn pictures that you can insert from the Microsoft Clip Gallery to visually enhance your presentation.

**Collapse**
In Outline View, reduces the selected slide to its title only, hiding all other text.

**Collapse All**
In Outline View, reduces all slides to their titles only, hiding all other text.

**Collate**
A printing option that instructs your computer to print one complete copy of a document before beggining the first page of the next copy.

**Color scheme**
The default colors assigned to basic aspects of a presentation such as text, background, and fill color.

**Common Tasks button**
Clicking this button opens a menu that offers three frequently used commands: New Slide, Slide Layout, and Apply Design Template.

**Contents tab**
A comprehensive help facility that organizes information by category.

**Crop**
To cut off portions of a graphic that you do not wish to display.

**Custom Animation**
A text or object movement, sometimes accompanied by sound, that animates a slide element in order to call attention to it or simply add to the overall effectiveness of the presentation.

## D

**Data series**
Data taken from a row or column of a datasheet.

**Datasheet**
A table of information that serves as a data source for creating a graphical chart.

**Demote**
To indent a line of text so that it is moved down a level in an outline hierarchy.

**Design Templates**
Prepared designs you can apply to presentation slides that include organizational patterns, formatting, and color schemes.

**Dialog box**
A box that explains the available command options for you to review or change before executing a command.

**Dotted border**
Indicates that the selected object can be resized or repositioned.

**Drag**
To hold down the mouse button while moving the mouse.

**Drive**
The mechanism in a computer that reads recordable media (such as a disk or tape cartridge) to retrieve and store information. Personal computers often have one hard disk drive labeled C, a drive that reads floppy disks labeled A, and a drive that reads CDs labeled D.

## E

**Elevation**
An option that allows you to change the angle at which you view a 3-D chart.

**Embedded object**
An object created in another application and then inserted in a PowerPoint presentation. Embedded objects can be linked to their original source for automatic updating.

**Expand**
In Outline View, reveals all of the selected slide's text if it has been collapsed previously.

**Expand All**
In Outline View, reveals all text on all slides if any of them have been collapsed previously.

## F

**Find and Replace**
Allows you to locate and edit specific instances of text without having to conduct a manual search.

**Folders**
Subdivisions of a disk that function as a filing system to help you organize files.

**Font**
A name given to a collection of text characters at a specific size, weight, and style. Arial and Times New Roman are examples of font names.

**Formatting toolbar**
Used to change the appearance of information on a slide. The Formatting toolbar contains shortcuts to the most common formatting commands.

## G

**Graph 2000**
The application used to create charts in PowerPoint.

**Grayscale Preview button**
Converts your presentation to shades of gray so you can see how it will appear when printed with a black and white printer.

# H

**Hashed border**
Indicates that the selected object can be resized, and that its contents, such as text, can be edited.

**HTML**
Programming language used to write Web pages. PowerPoint presentations can be saved as Web pages.

# I

**Index tab**
Organizes help topics in an alphabetical list.

**Insertion point**
A vertical blinking line on the screen that indicates where text and graphics will be inserted. The insertion point also indicates where an action will begin.

# L

**Legend**
Part of a chart that explains what each of the various data series markers represents.

# M

**Maximize**
To enlarge a window to its maximum size. Maximizing an application window causes it to fill the screen; maximizing a presentation window causes it to fill the application window.

**Menu bar**
Lists the names of menus containing PowerPoint commands. Click a menu name on the menu bar to display a list of commands.

**Microsoft Clip Gallery**
An index that contains tabs for storing Clip Art, pictures, sounds, and videos that you can insert into a presentation.

**Microsoft Clip Gallery Live**
A Microsoft Web page that provides additional clips that you can download to your computer. Your computer must be connected to the Internet to access this gallery.

**Microsoft Organization Chart**
The application you use to create an organization chart for a PowerPoint presentation slide.

**Minimize**
To shrink a window to its minimum size. Minimizing an application window reduces it to a button on the taskbar; minimizing a presentation window reduces it to a short title bar in the application window.

**More Buttons arrow**
Permits you to add buttons to a particular toolbar.

# N

**Normal View**
A tri-pane view that includes an outline pane, a slide pane, and notes pane, allowing you to work with different aspects of a presentation in the same window.

## Notes Page View

A PowerPoint view option that allows you to insert reference notes that you can use during a presentation or print out for the audience.

# O

## Objects

Lines, shapes, text boxes, clips, drawings, and other items you insert in a slide.

## Office Assistant

An animated representation of the Microsoft Office 2000 help facility. The Office Assistant provides hints, instructions, and a convenient interface between the user and PowerPoint's various help features.

## Open Copy

Command that opens a copy of the presentation you want to work with instead of the original file.

## Open in Browser

Command that allows you to open a presentation in your Web browser rather than in PowerPoint.

## Open Read-Only

Command that allows you to view a presentation, but not to make any permanent changes to it.

## Order command

Controls the order in which objects on the same slide are layered.

## Organization chart

A symbolic representation of a hierarchy or chain of command.

## Outline View

A PowerPoint view option that facilitates entering, editing, and arranging text that will appear on slides.

## Outlining toolbar

The toolbar available in Outline View that contains commands for promoting and demoting lines of text as well as for controlling what is visible in Outline View.

# P

## Pack and Go Wizard

Gathers all of the necessary elements of a presentation and compresses them so that they may be packaged onto a floppy disk for use elsewhere.

## Placeholder

A dashed border that designates where to insert specific objects.

## PowerPoint Viewer

A program that permits you to run a presentation on a computer that does not have PowerPoint installed.

## PowerPoint window

The window that contains the open PowerPoint application, and displays the PowerPoint menus, toolbars, and Presentation window.

## Presentation window

The main area of the PowerPoint window where you create, view, and edit your presentation.

## Promote

To move a line of text up a level in an outline hierarchy.

# R

**Resize**

To change the size of an object (such as a text box or graphic) by dragging the sizing handles located on its border. You can also adjust the dimensions of many objects from a dialog box.

**Right-click**

To click the right mouse button; often used to access specialized menus and shortcuts.

# S

**ScreenTip**

A brief explanation of a button or object that appears when the mouse pointer is paused over it. Other ScreenTips are accessed by using the What's This? feature on the Help menu or by clicking the question mark button in a dialog box.

**Scroll bar**

A graphical device for moving vertically or horizontally through a presentation with the mouse. Scroll bars are located along the right and bottom edges of the application window.

**Scroll bar box**

A small grey box located inside a scroll bar that indicates your current position relative to the rest of the presentation window. You can advance a scroll bar box by dragging it, clicking the scroll bar on either side of it, or by clicking the scroll arrows.

**Sizing handle**

A small square on the frame of an object that you can drag to resize the object. Sizing handles are generally located on the corners of a frame and at the midpoint of each of its sides.

**Slide icon**

A small rectangular symbol that rests next to the title of each presentation slide in Outline View.

**Slide Navigator**

Allows you to go to any slide in a presentation quickly during a slide show.

**Slide Show**

Runs your slides as they would appear during a presentation.

**Slide Show pop-up menu**

Menu that offers commands for working with a slide show. Can be opened by clicking the Slide Show pop-up menu icon or by right-clicking a slide.

**Slide Sorter View**

A PowerPoint view option that displays all slides simultaneously in miniature form. In Slide Sorter View you can rearrange slide order by dragging the miniatures and apply special effects to individual slides or groups of slides.

**Slide Transition effect**

A special effect that controls how a slide makes its appearance during a slide show. Slide transition timings can also be set.

## Slide Transition icon
A small slide symbol that appears beneath a slide in Slide Sorter view to indicate that a slide transition has been applied to that slide. Clicking the icon runs a preview of the transition effect.

## Slide View
A PowerPoint view option that facilitates creating, modifying, and enhancing individual slides.

## Standard toolbar
The row of buttons just below the menu bar that performs the most basic and most commonly used commands in PowerPoint.

## Status bar
Provides information about your current position in a presentation at the bottom of the PowerPoint window. The type of information changes depending on the view you are in.

## Style Checker
A PowerPoint feature that checks your presentation for visual clarity, case, and end punctuation.

## Summary slide
A slide that summarizes an entire presentation by presenting all of the presentation's slide titles as a bulleted list.

# T

## Text box
A rectangular area in which text is added so that it may be manipulated independently. Can also refer to a box inside a dialog box where you enter information necessary to execute a command.

## Text label box
A text box created by clicking with the Text Box tool. Text in this type of box does not wrap to the next line when it reaches the edge of the box. Text label boxes are best used for single words or short phrases.

## Timing
The amount of time a slide remains in view before a slide show advances to the next slide. Animation effects also have timings to control when they occur.

## Timing icon
In Slide Sorter View, displays the amount of time a slide will remain on the screen before the presentation advances to the next slide.

## Title bar
The horizontal bar at the top of the window that displays the name of the document or application that appears in the window.

## Title slide
A slide AutoLayout, generally used for the first slide in a presentation.

## Toolbar
A graphical bar containing buttons that act as shortcuts for common application commands.

# U

## Undo command
Reverse the last action you performed. The Undo button includes a drop-down list of all your recent actions so that you may undo multiple operations.

## V

**View Datasheet button**
Toggles the Datasheet window on and off when you are working in Microsoft Graph 2000.

## W

**What's This?**
A help feature that allows you to click on a screen item in order to receive a ScreenTip that explains the item.

**Window**
A rectangular area on the screen in which you view and work on files.

**Wizard**
A series of specialized dialog boxes that walks you through the completion of certain tasks.

**WordArt**
Text that is inserted as a drawing object, allowing it to be manipulated and formatted as an object rather than as standard text.

**Word processing text box**
A text box created by clicking and dragging with the Text Box tool. A word processing box allows text to wrap to the next line when it reaches the edge of the box and is useful for longer sentences and passages of text.

## Z

**Zoom box**
Allows you to "zoom in" on your work for easier viewing.

# Index

## U

## V

## W

## X

## Z

Notes • Notes